PRAISE FOR 21 MYTHS (EVEN GOOD) GIRLS BELIEVE ABOUT SEX

"Jennifer Strickland writes with honesty, experience, passion, and sensitivity in this important book. *21 Myths (Even Good) Girls Believe about Sex* lists the lies the enemy wants to imprint on the hearts and minds of girls and then follows up with life-giving truths that cleanse, transform, and heal faulty thinking. This book should be read by every teenage girl, but it will also bring renewed hope to women of all ages who have allowed past wrong choices to keep them in spiritual and mental bondage. I highly recommend this resource!"
–Carol Kent, Speaker and Author,
Becoming a Woman of Influence (NavPress)

"Authentic and truth-filled, *21 Myths (Even Good) Girls Believe about Sex* is a relevant reminder of God's design for sex, love, and intimacy. Jennifer shows us in practical ways how to pursue passion and purity while living winsomely in the world, yet not of the world. As a mom of two tween daughters, this resource will be a 'go-to' for many years to come. Highly recommended!"
—Cindy Bultema, Women's Speaker,
Bible Teacher, and Author of *Red Hot Faith*

"In a culture that seeks to convince us sexual purity is an antiquated philosophy, Jennifer Strickland proves the opposite. In *21 Myths (Even Good) Girls Believe about Sex*, she uncovers the lies that would have us believe purity of mind and body stands in the way of our sexual freedoms. Through candid stories, analogies, and personal transparency she reveals the truth about sex—that purity does not inhibit physical pleasure but liberates us to enjoy sex the way it was designed to be. . .pleasure without pain or remorse."
—Tracey Mitchell, Speaker,
TV Host, and Author of *Downside Up*

"Candid, honest, straigh   art that tenderly and truthfully ca   · Strick-land tackles the much-n   :omfort and ease of sitting with a   es truth and beauty into the read

—Pam Farrel, Author of *Red Hot Monogamy*,
52 Ways to Wow Your Husband: Put a Smile on His Face
and *Red Hot Romance Tips for Women*

"This is the book I've been waiting for. *21 Myths* answers the questions women have but haven't dared to speak aloud. Jennifer has done the hard work, and all you need to do is pick it up. I'm going to read it to my three teens tonight at the dinner table!"
—Margot Starbuck, Author of *Unsqueezed*

"Jennifer's latest is as much about love as it is about sex. That's good, because love is what we're *really* after! *21 Myths* is an honest, grace-soaked, truth-filled addition to modern discussions about intimacy."
—Jessie Minassian, Author of *Crushed: Why Guys Don't Have to Make or Break.You* and *Backwards Beauty: How to Feel Ugly in 10 Simple Steps*

"This book is Jennifer's best yet, capturing and explaining the true essence of the longings of our hearts and how to have those longings fulfilled, God's Way. . . . Jennifer gives practical wisdom and step-by-step guidance that can heal girls and women of any age and background from the pain and confusion that they have experienced in the area of love and sexuality and give them renewed hope and purpose so that they can experience the fullness of God's love, regardless of what they have been through."
—Laurel A. Slade, MS, BCPCC, LMHC, LMFT

"As someone who has literally been on the inside of the media machine as a model for famous designers, Jennifer knows what she's talking about when it comes to battling media messages and replacing them with God's truth. I highly recommend her work!"
—Constance Rhodes, Founder and CEO, FINDINGbalance, Inc; Author, *More Than a Number: Why Who You Are Is Already Enough*

"Jennifer Strickland writes with compelling conviction about sexuality. Her caring heart and incredible love story compel her to tell the truth about sex—the good and the bad. Her candid approach, spiritual sensitivity, and insightful writing create a plumb line for young women to follow."
—Devi Titus, Author. Speaker. Mentor. Kingdom Global Ministries

"Jennifer raises the bar for us to believe in God's truth versus the current cultural lies about genuine beauty, self-worth, and true love. . . . My prayer is that all girls would read *21 Myths (Even Good) Girls Believe about Sex* and pursue the safe pasture of God's perfect boundary lines—a beautiful place where true love has always been intended to stay."

—Annie Pajcic, ThouArtExalted Ministries,
www.ThouArtExalted.com

"I wish someone had handed me this guidepost the day I turned fifteen. Jennifer Strickland candidly and authentically delivers a hard-hitting and refreshing message about the beauty and integrity of God's design for sex, which every girl and young woman need to hear."

—Allie Marie Smith,
Founder of Wonderfully Made, Author

"This book exposes real lies about sex faced by girls of all ages and provides the honest biblical truth they need to move from a life of disillusionment, hurt, and disappointment to one of hope, healing, purity, and real LOVE."

—Reverend Trina Titus Lozano, Counselor and Founder,
Wait, the Smart Choice

"When I read the first few pages of this powerful, positive, progressive, palatable truth, I promised myself that all my children, grandchildren, and many friends would get a copy because this conversation can clear our minds about the true essence of sex!"

—Professor Thelma Wells, D.D.,
Master's International University of Divinity,
CEO That A Girl Enrichment, Speaker, Author

"*21 Myths* is grace-filled, honest, and overflows with love. The insight and wisdom into the forbidden topic of sex opens the door for REAL conversation that renews, restores, and redeems hope, joy, beauty, and trust."

–Debbie Eaton, Champion and Coach to the Next Generation
of Women through Writing, Speaking, and Connecting
over a Good Cup of Coffee and a Piece of Chocolate;
Former Director of Women's Ministry, Saddleback Church

Dedication

For my husband, the Cowboy.
Shane, this message is the incense of the love
we share. With your strong arms around me,
you have shown me the gentle nature of passion
and romance. You are my best friend, my lover,
and my husband—and you have uncovered for
me the true beauty of love and desire—
through promises that last. I am so
grateful that all of me is yours.
I love you, forever and always.
xoxoxo, Jen

21 MYTHS (EVEN GOOD)
Girls Believe About
Sex

PURSUING LOVE WITH PASSION + PURITY

Jennifer Strickland

SHILOH RUN PRESS
An Imprint of Barbour Publishing, Inc.

He has made everything beautiful in its time.

ECCLESIASTES 3:11 NIV

CONTENTS

INTRODUCTION

When the idea for this book first came to me, I knew I could write it. But I could not have guessed how it would change me as a person.

This book is about sexual integrity, based on the premise that preserving your body means preserving your heart—and giving your body means giving your soul.

I am a girl who has been saved, healed, and delivered by love, and love keeps changing me for the better. "21 Myths about Sex" is really "21 Truths about Love," for love is what we're really after.

21 Myths will help you:

- ♡ learn about love and what it looks like in all its parts and pieces

- ♡ embrace sex as God designed, free from guilt and shame

- ♡ heal from a broken past and live freely in grace and truth

- ♡ protect your sexuality, your body, your health, and your heart

- ♡ enhance your understanding of the true meaning of sex as the fabric of a loving marriage

When I first started writing, I thought the topic would be sex, but in the end I discovered it was about so much more. Ultimately, this is a book about love. It's about knowing someone so fully that you love him not only in between the sheets but in the ups and downs, in the valley and on the mountaintop, and you love forever, the way God loves us.

In writing, I discovered sex has to do with patience, kindness, forgiveness, and humility. It isn't just physical; it is spiritual and emotional. It isn't just temporary; it is lasting. And it isn't brief; it is bonding. It is the calling and completion of the married couple to be woven together for a lifetime.

There are things that surprised me about this book. Sex is not like a double-sided coin you can flip over, flat on each side. Instead, it is more like a diamond that appears different when illumined by various kinds of light. It's a topic that encompasses babies, health, heartbreak, shame, abuse, homosexuality, media, pornography, body image, prostitution, dating, marriage, God, scripture, truth, and of course love. It's highly multidimensional and very interesting!

I honestly can't think of a subject more daring than sex. I wrote scared most of the time, but because my story is a love story, I had the power to write it. The topic of sex unveils for us love in all its angles. It is a mystery and a marvelous gift. But the world has made it dicey. Dangerous. Tragic. Treacherous. I don't know of a subject more intriguing than this short, simple word, with three letters.

Sex. Even the word can send shivers down the spine of a teenage boy and send giggling girls running for cover. We can host whole parties for virgin brides (with lingerie galore) celebrating the beauty and majesty of sex, and we can go through thousands of tissues for the girls damaged and degraded by sex.

Sadly, even the thought of sex can usher in dark, shadowy memories for girls who gave away too early what should have been saved for later. Others are riddled by shame and remorse because someone else didn't protect or respect their bodies. For those who have been sexually abused, the word *sex* conjures up physical and emotional trauma, the likes of which we don't even want to imagine. Sex combined with abuse calls forth demons we'd rather keep quiet, but brokenhearted women cry out in the night, tears streaming down their faces.

The word *sex* brings to life scenes from movies, full of romance and allure. Sex ignites desire. The longing to be loved, held, and known is a force so strong that it can seem—although it's not—impossible to restrain. Physical touch can bring comfort and healing or pain and regret. When known from duty or by force, sex can leave us feeling unsatisfied and empty, used and discarded, shamed and confused. When enjoyed in the sanctuary of the pure bedsheets of a loving marriage, sex is heavenly.

———

When I was a teen, I needed this book. I needed an honest-to-goodness conversation on the corner couch at Starbucks about the complexities of sex and the true meaning of it.

21 Myths is that Starbucks conversation, me and you. I'm going to be real with you (because conversations about sex must be honest). I'd better warn you now, though: I'm not going to hold back telling you the truth on this all-too-important topic.

My goal?

♡ *If you haven't become sexually active yet:* My hope is to equip you to win the battle for your chastity and be a virgin bride for your husband. But I'm not going to promise you a prince or that it's going to be easy! I am also not going to promise you that people are going to agree with you, but I am going to help you! I'll give you the who, what, when, where, and why, and I'll teach you what the Bible says about sex, and you are going to love it!

♡ *If you're sexually active outside of marriage and feel guilty, ashamed, or unsure:* My goal is to help you heal and move on to a better road, where love and desire meet faithfulness and commitment; out-of-control meets self-control; passion meets purity; and purity means good, solid relationships for you. Ultimately, my goal is that you walk whole, strong, powerful, and free!

♡ *If you're sexually active outside of marriage and don't feel one bit bad about it:* My intention is not to make you feel bad about it! But I'd like the opportunity to guide you into God's best for you when it comes to your body, health, and future. I liken it to holding on to semiprecious stones when God has precious stones for you. Sometimes we hold on to something semiprecious because it has value and we really like it. But if we let go of what is semiprecious—if we open our hands—God can drop the diamonds into our palms. So hang with me and let's see if this new painting of sex is what your heart really longs for.

♡ *If you're married:* I hope to inspire you to understand that true sexual intimacy is possible and something you can strive for and grow in. I also want us to be as direct as possible about the complexities of sex when talking to our daughters, sons, and their friends—because they need the real deal from us, and that's what this book dishes out.

I invite you to use this book in the best way it suits you. You can look up myths and read them out of order, which I encourage. Or read it cover to cover with a girlfriend, mentor, or lamp! I kind of like the "in order" choice, because brushstroke by brushstroke, we are going to paint a new picture of sex as we know it. But it's up to you. (And when you are done with this book, just leave it on the table at the local coffee shop, sorority house, gyno's office, or wherever women and girls go, okay? Okay. Deal.)

Imagine a sky after a long storm: washed, radiant, brushstrokes that paint a sunrise in blasts of color over a canvas swept clean. That's my life. At one time, I knew shame and let its shadows nearly swallow me alive. But then I encountered the love of Christ. From then on, it was God's love that changed me and transformed the way I live in this body.

Today I know love in its tenderest sense, and I want that for you. I want you to know the simplicity of love between the sheets that has been blessed by the Father and celebrated by heaven. I want you to know passion with purity, the true beauty of love and desire.

Why else would I attempt to write a book on sex? I'm certainly not writing for me. I am writing for you, because I have seen far too many tearstained faces from girls hurt too young. I've also peered deep into too many women's faces bitter with regret, aged too soon, because sex hasn't been fair to them either. And I know you don't want any of that, no matter your age! I know you want the dream and the destiny, love unrestrained and beautiful. So *you* are my why for this book—you are my why.

Look, there is good sex and bad sex, and I want you to understand the difference and choose the good,

> *I want you to know the simplicity of love between the sheets that has been blessed by the Father and celebrated by heaven. I want you to know passion <u>with</u> purity, the <u>true beauty of love and desire</u>.*

like I did on my wedding day. And when I picked good, I got *great*.

Twenty-one myths. Twenty-one truths. Take hold of them. I pray they bless you the way they have blessed me. Let's pretend like we're whispering over coffee on the corner couch, just me and you!

MYTH 1:

Sex Is Bad, and
Only Bad Girls Want Sex.

(Sex is shameful. Shhhh, don't talk about it!)

TRUTH 1:

Sex Is Good, and
Good Girls Want Sex.

(It's how we go about it that can be good or bad.)

LIFE VERSE:

*[Jesus] stood up and said to them,
"Let him who is without sin among you be
the first to throw a stone at her."*

JOHN 8:7 ESV

Time to get down to business. First, we gotta knock out the lie in the title of this book. Yep, I slipped a myth into the title, and I gotta come clean about it. Honestly, I did it for you, because you probably think you are either a *good girl or a bad girl.*

From now on I promise I'll stick with the truth until I tell you otherwise. First of all, you are not "good" or "bad," and neither is the hooker on the corner. The girl who has sex before marriage is not a bad person. The girl who has had an abortion is not a bad person. The girl who struggles with homosexual thoughts is not a bad person. The pregnant teen is not bad; the rape victim—nope, not her either. The girl everyone calls "slut" at school. . .and the one who cheats on her husband—their actions may be harmful, but nope, we're not going to label them shameful or bad in this book. Our good God loves these girls just as much as He loves the girls who are walking in sexual integrity, so let's just establish that from the beginning.

I don't consider myself a good girl or a bad girl. I consider myself a girl who was lost and confused, who got hurt and hurt herself, and hurt others. At my worst, I cried out for real, lasting love; and over time, I received the answer to my prayers.

I do not consider myself an expert on the topic of sex, but I am a girl who had a torn and confused soul, who has been healed of my past, and who has received grace in waves that lap on the shore of my heart. I am no better and no worse than the lady sitting next to me in church, silently crying over her husband's rejection, or the college girl with her heels dangling in her hand, walking home from a late night of partying. Our stories may seem different, but at heart we are the same: we all want a love that is lasting, that endures, that fills us up instead of empties us out.

Any girl who gives her body away for free or sells it for a price pays the toll. And any woman distraught because the man she wants doesn't want her—she hurts. We are all God's "loved" girls no matter what—and we've all got to learn to live from that place of identity. We are God's beloved daughters—and everything we do in our bodies flows from that.

So what qualifies me to write this book? Well, my husband and I have chosen to follow God's design for sex, and there is peace and security there. My husband's name is Shane, and in previous books that's what I've called him. But from here on out, I'll refer to him as the Cowboy, simply because he won my California heart with his Southern charm and moved me to Texas to love me forever. (And because he looks awfully sexy on a tractor.)

The Sex Symbol

Let's make one thing clear: sex is not bad, and the desire for sex is not bad. In fact, sex can be the most delicious and delightful experience two people can have together. The desire for sex is normal, healthy, and good. In marriage, this desire develops a beautiful bond between two people. Like two magnets, sex bonds a husband and wife into spiritual, emotional, and physical oneness. That bond is so strong that they can face and fight the fiercest storms of life as *one*.

In a great marriage, sex is a salve that heals our wounded hearts. Sex a way to accept one another in all our faults. Sex is a symbol of forgiveness, grace, and love.

The media presents a "sex symbol" as someone who is to be lusted after—someone who joins his or her body with others carelessly, who represents the lust of the flesh and a feast for the eyes.

How opposite this is to the symbol God uses for sex! In God's design, sex is a symbol for oneness, not for many eyes, many hearts, many bodies. Sex symbolizes unity between Christ and the church, between God and His people, between a man and woman in marriage.

God has given us one directive on life—the Bible. It is the source for all wisdom and truth. It is God-breathed. His Word is flawless and gives us direction on how to treat people, our bodies, our relationships, and our money, how to find our mission in life—and it has a lot to say about sex. It has so much to say that I fear I cannot encompass it all in one book. And it's true, I can't. But what I can do is tell you everything I know about the truths and lies when it comes to sex and offer this book as a gift for your heart.

I hope to do one of three things for you:

♥ help you see the real beauty of love and desire, sex through God's eyes

♥ free and heal you from lies you've believed about sex and your body

♥ inspire you to embrace sex in the fullness of your marriage bed

In my marriage, it has occurred to me that two people spending their lives together requires compromise, grace, and dedication. It also requires an appreciation for each other's differences and the ability to make music together. The Cowboy and I are so different. When he works out, he jams to hard rock; and no matter how hard I'm running, I listen to worship. But together we make country, and we have a whole lot of heart and soul. Sex for us is a place where we come together as one.

Sex is mysterious and marvelous, healing and heavenly. Sex unifies us, teaches us to let go of differences and disputes and love each other with the flavor of grace, the sweetest taste of anything in all the world. Holy sex is a cornucopia for our souls, offering deep inward healing and releasing our bodies from negativity and pain. Sex experienced God's way leaves no trace of shame, shadow of regret, or residue of past mistakes. Instead, good sex, or you might say, "God sex," cleanses and heals and empowers us to love selflessly, wholly, the way Christ loves us. Whereas sex outside of marriage wounds people, God's design for sex within marriage is to heal and make whole.

Oh, the wonders of sex! It is the physical symbol of the spiritual union of man and wife, the communion of our sole unity with God. It is so beautiful I could burst, but I won't do that because we are just getting going.

A Very Bad, No Good, Thing

Can you imagine an entire crowd ready to kill you right in front of Jesus?

I cannot imagine that. But I can imagine this: if everyone wanted to kill me, I know the first person I'd want invited to that party: Jesus!

Like anything, sex can be used for good or for evil.

But not like anything, sexual sin is superpersonal. It's not quite like lying, cheating, stealing, or destroying property, but it does lead to lying, cheating, stealing, and destroying property.

Let's take, for example, the woman from the Bible who gets caught cheating on her husband, in our life verse for this myth. This woman feels embarrassed, humiliated, and ashamed—especially since her adultery has gone public— kind of like when a girl's sexting gets passed around to the entire senior class, then to the juniors, sophomores, and freshmen too. And the administration, who then let her parents know, and even with that, her "best friend" can't keep quiet about it, so the whole town

> But not like anything, sexual sin is superpersonal. It's not quite like lying, cheating, stealing, or destroying property, but it does lead to lying, cheating, stealing, and destroying property.

knows—oh yes, and all her followers on Twitter too. She'll be lucky if it doesn't get splashed on her Instagram page before she crawls into a hole and wants to stay there forever.

First of all, this "bad girl of the Bible" who got caught cheating on her husband has all this pain to begin with since she went outside of her marriage. Driven by her natural desires for affection and love, or driven by forces of attraction and lust, she fell. We don't know the complexities of her marriage or why her longings led her to this forsaken place. But we do know this: humans struggle; humans fall. I've known a few women who fell into adultery, and as far as I can tell, their stories match that of Eve's.

Something looks good, tastes good. . .and they believe it's going to make them feel better, so they get duped into believing it *is* good, but in truth it separates them from their families and God, and they pay the penalty. So it goes with all sin. All fall.

It's interesting that the religious leaders are ready to slam her to the ground for her sin. Not only do they want to watch the bloody mess, but they are positioned to cause it. Will it somehow make them feel better? Humph. That's why I'd want Jesus at my stoning party; and by a stroke of destiny for this woman, He is.

Not much in life is kept secret for long, and this woman is stricken by terror. The whipped-cream-gone-bad on top of her sundae of shame is the wrath of death by stoning at the hands of the very people she thought she respected—the religious community. The Old Testament law of Moses required people caught in adultery to be stoned—a law we never see fulfilled—so she is our first example.

There she is, surrounded by the mob of prideful men.

This woman has done a very-bad-awful-no-good thing, so we may be tempted to call her by the name of her sin—adulteress, whore, dirty slut. For she is the "offender," the "offensive one." Or are we named by our sin? Do you want to be called by the name of your sin?

With a crowd of people taunting Him, Jesus stoops down on the ground and begins writing with His finger. He stoops to her level—down in the dirt. No one knows what He wrote that day, but I'd take a shot at Revelation 2:17 ESV: "To the one who conquers I will give. . .a new name written. . .that no one knows except the one who receives it."

And the prophecy of Isaiah comes true:

> *"For the LORD has called you like a wife deserted and grieved in spirit, like a wife of youth when she is cast off, says your God. For a brief moment I deserted you, but with great compassion I will gather you. In overflowing anger for a moment I hid my face from you, but with everlasting love I will have compassion on you. . . .*
>
> *You shall be called by a new name that the mouth of the LORD will give. You shall be a crown of beauty in the hand of the LORD, and a royal diadem in the hand of your God. You shall no more be termed Forsaken, and your land shall no*

*more be termed Desolate, but you shall be called
My Delight Is in Her, and your land Married; for
the Lord delights in you, and your land shall be
married. . . . For as. . .the bridegroom rejoices
over the bride, so shall your God rejoice over
you. (Isaiah 54:6–8; 62:2–5 ESV, emphasis added)*

I bet He writes her new name in the earth. Maybe it is Chosen One. Forgiven. Cherished. Loved. But it is certainly not Deserted. Degraded. Shamed. Damned.

When the pesky Pharisees keep badgering Him with questions, Jesus stands up to them, challenging them to look in the mirror. "The one without sin among you should be the first to throw a stone at her" (John 8:7 HCSB).

The more they consider their own histories, the more quickly they drop their rocks.

Have you ever done a very-bad-awful-no-good thing?

Just checking. Because I have. In fact, I have done a lot of very-bad-awful-no-good things, and I'd really rather not be named by them—by you or anybody else, and especially by God. So I'm not going to pick up my rock to aim it at anybody.

If you have fallen, I will come down to where you are in the dirt and let you know you're not alone. I'm not going to throw any rocks at you.

If you've had sex with many people, one person, or have a hidden sin—you are loved. If you have been a sex addict, a sex slave, sexually abused, addicted to porn, had one or more abortions, cheated on your husband or boyfriend, experienced homosexual relations, lied to your parents or friends, lied to yourself or to God,

Have you ever done a very-bad-awful-no-good thing?

you are loved. And I'm going to stand up right here and tell the world to look in the mirror—and maybe, just maybe, if they are really honest, they will drop their rocks.

Bottom line about this woman: she is not condemned—otherwise, Jesus would have said so. The only one allowed to condemn is the One who has no sin, and He offers grace.

"Woman. . .has no one condemned you?" (*Woman* means "life," so this is a sweet term of endearment.)

"No one, Lord," she answers.

"Neither do I condemn you; go, and from now on sin no more."[1]

In this story, God is the good one, and the accusers are the bad ones. Not her. Not you. You are neither good nor bad—you are just forgiven.

There is not one biblical record where Jesus heaps shame upon a woman; in every case, He first releases her from shame.

So this is the way we are going to start the conversation about sex.

You, *and* that girl at school being called a "slut," *and* that woman you know who cheated—are not condemned. That means if you put your trust in Christ, your slate is clean. If there has been any sexual sin in your past, give it to Him and receive His forgiveness.

And then get up and shake off the dirt. We've got places to go.

Good Girls Have Sex

Good girls have sex. Yes, they do, and it really bugs me when the church acts like they don't—like you pass from

---

1. John 8:10–11 ESV

"good" to "bad" the moment you have intercourse. That is such a lie! There are good *choices* and bad *choices*—good and bad *consequences*—and we are going to cover them when it comes to sex.

But the first truth is, (even good) girls fall.

Good girls want sex, and they should, because we were created for it—our name, Woman, means "life."

Life can only come from one place—the woman's womb.

Life is born from sex.

So sex is good, and your desire for it is good too.

God saw all that he had created, and said, it is good.
And after he made Eve, he called it "very good!"[2]

2. Genesis 1:25, 31

MYTH 2:

If I've Already Been Sexually Active,
It's Too Late for Me to Be Pure.

(So I might as well give up.)

—

TRUTH 2:

Forgiveness Purifies You.

(Don't let the dirt stick.)

LIFE VERSE:

"Everyone who drinks of this water will be thirsty again, but whoever drinks of the water that I will give him will never be thirsty again."

JOHN 4:13–14 ESV

The Mud Pit

When it rains, dirt can turn into mud or quicksand. There's dirt you roll around in because it looks like fun. I did this once. I went to a concert in a huge field, and a rainstorm pummeled the crowd. People got so muddy, they started dancing and sloshing around in the mud until almost everyone dove in and got mud plastered. Finally, my girlfriend and I joined the craze and played slip and slide. We ended up wearing a giant mud mask from head to toe and took a bunch of funny pictures. It was fun and crazy, and all it took was a long shower to wash it off and a trash can for our clothes!

With sex, a lot of people jump in willfully because it looks like fun. The hotties seem to be quite happy rolling about in it. So why wouldn't we be happy too?

If it were all well and good, why don't the hotties go home and tell their dads about rolling around naked with the guy who picked them up at 7:00? Or why when they see the guy in class, can they barely look him in the eye now? Or why do they find themselves sitting on the sidewalk outside his fraternity house crying because he moved away? Sex can look, sound, and taste superyummy, and it feels good at the time, so people jump. But they get all muddy—and then they try to hide the mud, but this kind of mud sticks.

A shower can't wash off this kind of mud. Not even a really long, hot one.

In the Garden

The very unique thing about sex outside of marriage (this is basic sex 101 here) is that you "carry it around in your body." Sexual sin is not like lying or cheating. It actually becomes a part of you. When you have sex with someone, you become one with that person, which is how babies are made. Two distinct individuals join to form one body (Genesis 2:24). Man plus woman equals child.

This is simple biology. It's not manmade. We couldn't change it if we tried; and believe me, man has tried to change the law of creation, and he's still trying. Who would argue that two male dogs make a dog? Science proves this. A male dog joined with a female dog equals a cute little puppy, period. Trying to make a new way to create life will only make your head hurt. It is what it is; just as the sun comes up in the morning and the moon lights the night, God created us male and female, and together we are a reflection of Him.

In creation God distinguishes between the two. First He created light, marking the difference between day and night; then He separated water and sky; dry land and sea; seed-bearing plants and fruit-bearing trees; then two great lights—the sun to govern the day and the moon to govern the night, and the stars. Then He differentiated between the creatures of the air and the creatures of the sea. Next He made livestock, creepy crawly things, and wild animals, each according to their kind.

Last, He made "man in his own image, in the image of God he created him; male and female he created them" (Genesis 1:27 ESV). He distinguished between night and day, land and sea, moon and sun, male and female. He created us according to our kind, and once He did that, He said, *Now this is very good! Go and reproduce.*

Our *first* command was to be fruitful and multiply and increase in number. How is that done? Sex.

"For this reason a man shall leave his father and his mother, and be joined to his wife; and they shall become one flesh. And the man and his wife were both naked and were not ashamed" (Genesis 2:24–25 NASB).

There is no shame in sex when it is experienced in marriage. But somewhere along the line, our culture has convinced us that God's design was wrong. He messed up. He didn't really mean what He said. He meant to say "boyfriend" and "girlfriend" instead of "man" and "wife."

But as sure as he said "night" and "day," he said "man" and "wife."

Not "woman." Not "girl." But "wife."

What happened when the first couple disobeyed God's command and ate from the one tree He guarded them from, the tree of the knowledge of good and evil? Words like *hiding, fear, deceit, cursed, hostility, pain, anguish,* and *murder* entered the scene—replacing the words *good, very good, light, fruitful, life, pleasing, flowing,* and *blessed.*

Yikes.

One Flesh

The first record of Adam and Eve having sex is in Genesis 4:1, when Adam "knew" (ESV) his wife Eve and she conceived and gave birth to their son. The word for "knew" is *yada*—and it is means a deep, emotional knowing and mutual respect, an understanding between the two.[1]

It is the same word used for, "Be still, and *know* that I am God" (Psalm 46:10 ESV) and "Search me, O God, and *know* my heart" (Psalm 139:23).

In other words, Adam *knew* Eve's heart. He *understood* her. He *respected her deeply.* He *knew* her emotionally.

1. Dannah Gresh, *What Are You Waiting For?: The One Thing No One Ever Tells You about Sex* (Colorado Springs: Waterbrook, 2011), 17.

And she conceived.

At the point of conception (sperm meets egg), the seed of new life begins. That seed is eternal, just as you are eternal. God breathed His life into you as He knit you together in your mother's womb and saw your unformed body as He wove you together in the depths of the earth (Psalm 139:13–15 NIV). When He created Adam, we read: "The LORD God. . .breathed the breath of life into the man's nostrils, and the man became a living person" (Genesis 2:7).

The creation of new life is the most mysterious and beautiful mystery on the earth. What's even more magical is when the mother and father *know* each other as man and wife. Through marriage, they have committed to lay a secure foundation for that child to grow into his dreams and destiny as a child of God.

That child has a soul. The mother is tied to the child; the father is tied to the child. There is also a tie between the mother and father, even if a baby was not created in the union, for they became "one."

Sexual arousal causes the hormone dopamine to be released into the brain, which washes your brain with peace and pleasure. This is a chemical that makes you want more, more, more. Whether it is more drugs, more sex, more alcohol, or more love, you want it. Dopamine pours emotional glue over the source that has brought you pleasure. It's addictive.

In the case of man and wife, this is perfect! The more pleasure experienced in the marriage bed, the more joyful their relationship will be; the more bonded they will feel. Their tie will create a glue-like bond that will help keep the family together through thick and thin.

Heart Break, Soul Ache

In the case of two unmarried people, we end up with a bond, a craving, and a longing for more that is not secure. Either one of them is free to break that bond.

When one of them breaks the bond, there is a ripping in the soul.

The heart rips. The brain aches. The longing for what we cannot have is heart-wrenching. Despair, depression, and emptiness bring angst to the soul.

Soul ties are not easily broken and cannot be washed off with water.

You can't take off the clothes and throw them in the trash.

Your heart is bonded.

Your fluids have mixed.

Your flesh has joined.

You have become one.

There's not a shower in the world that can wash that away.

Let's say he is seventeen. You are sixteen—and you don't want to get married till maybe twenty-four? That's eight years away! And he attends a different college than you do.

Or he's twenty-six, and you are twenty-four. Still. . .

He moves on to graduate school.

He doesn't want to be tied down.

He's not ready to support a family.

He meets another girl and falls in love.

But he's still not ready for "commitment."

But you. . .

committed already.

You gave him:

your virginity.

your body.

your heart.

the most vulnerable part of you.

You are:

        afraid you might be pregnant.

        carrying his child. . .

        or for the rest of your life, sharing his disease,
which wreaks havoc on your genitals year after year.

You have:

        his herpes.

        his heart.

        his dreams.

You ache for him:

        to want you.

        to tell you that he's sorry and he does love
you and wants to marry you. . .

        but he doesn't.

        he graduates.

        he picks the other girl.

        or he wants you to get an abortion.

But no matter what you do,

        he doesn't. . .

            want. . .

                you. . .

So. . .

    your heart slowly sews over the wound.

Then. . .

    you fall in love again.

        You really think he's the one.

        You really think so.

        He says he loves you.

You think he *knows* you. *Respects* you. *Adores* you.

        But he doesn't call you the next day.

        Then the day you fear comes:

        he leaves.

You cry,
and hope he'll come back.
But he doesn't.
You hurt—
real bad.
Your heart
gives way.
Next time it's easier to give your body away because. . .
your purity is gone—
so what does it matter
now?

Every lie starts with a seed. The seed takes on life the more you water it. Here's the lie: it's too late for me to be pure anyway.

And we don't just believe lies. We live them out.

Quicksand

There's this other kind of mud—the kind we wish we didn't have to talk about. It's the slippery slime someone shoves you into. You didn't want to get in. You were cruising along in life. You had your own set of demons—everybody does—but you weren't partnering with them. Until they took you out when no one was looking.

You were drinking at a party. Or someone slipped a drug in your water. You were on a date. You were walking home. You were at a concert. You were on vacation, and you trusted the wrong guy. Or worse, you were a child, when beds and bathrooms were supposed to be safe places.

The enemy came from behind, took you by the nape of your neck, and shoved your face in the mud. Your nose clogged; your mouth too. You couldn't breathe. You squirmed, you fought, you froze. He kept sloshing your face around in the thick, wet muck and broke open your insides. Rape was violent, cruel, the blackest evil. Or a slow, subtle, agonizing manipulation until he convinced you wrong was right and right was wrong and dark was light and dark was good.

Hard, angry, mean man.

Slow, lying trickery.

Dirty, rotten, ruined girl.

Scared, lonely, broken child.

Maybe it happened once. Or it happened again and again. But you know this: you didn't want in this pit, and now it's sucking you down. Every time you want to climb out, it grips you. Every time you get your head above the surface, the mud gets in your mouth and in your ears and in your eyes and you try to gasp for breath and your mouth is clogged and a big, huge, hurt part of you wants to let go and keep sinking and let the blackest muck swallow you dead alive.

But there's this light, this truth, and you know it deep down: you are not a dirty girl, a bad girl; you are a loved girl, and that truth is woven inside your heart.

From the quicksand, sinking, you see a shaft of sunbeam, and it pierces the mud dark. Out of the corner of your eye you see it, and you reach for it.

Then, an arm, strong and mighty. Its grip is faithful and fierce, and you take it.

You hold on tight.

He lifts you.

God.

You see the face of a woman. Or the arm of a man. Someone who is willing to get dirty to help you see you're not.

This is someone who saw you before and knows: you were woven together in the depths of your mother's womb by the God of all creation, and He stitched dreams into your soul. Bedazzled purpose. Designed a plan.

He calls you friend. Treasure. Pearl.

He whispers sweet air into your lungs: you are More. His words breathe life into you. You are More than your worst moment, this sin, your dark night. You are His, and He's taking you back and giving you a new name: "Mine."

The Living Water

Try as we may, we can't wash wounds away with a shower.

Yet there is an internal cleansing we can receive by the power of the Holy Spirit, for Jesus said that streams of living water would flow from within (John 4:14).

You know who He said this to?

A woman with an empty bucket. A woman like you and me. A woman who hid her shame, concealed her pain, and was looking to men to fill the bucket of her soul.

At a time when people wouldn't cross her path, she came to the well at midday to draw water. We wonder if she came at that time to avoid the glares, the stares, the judgment of those who condemned her for her race or her reputation. "'You are a Jew and I am a Samaritan woman. How can you ask me for a drink?'" (For Jews do not associate with Samaritans.) (John 4:9 NIV).

Kind of like "Blacks don't associate with Mexicans."
Kind of like "Prostitutes don't show up at Bible study."
Kind of like that.

(For the record, I know these statements are false. I'm

pinpointing cultural lies that keep people from knowing one another and knowing God. I actually really like people of all shapes, sizes, and colors! Most of my events are filled with people from many backgrounds and walks of life. And one of my favorite friends is an ex-prostitute who eats, drinks, and breathes Bible study.)

But *this* woman was not to associate with Jews—that was unheard of in her day. So was divorce. So was sex outside of marriage. She was about to get her cup dumped inside out.

Far from her mind would have been the thought that she was going to bump into the Savior of her hurting heart. But there He was. . .Jesus sitting at the well.

He asked her for a cup of water, and she quickly pointed out their differences. "You: Jew. Me: Samaritan. We no talk."

Then He offered her a gift: the living water.

"Where can you get this living water?" she asked.

"Whoever drinks the water I give them will never thirst," He said. "Indeed, the water I give them will become in them a spring of water welling up to eternal life."

"Sir, give me this water. . ." she said.

Then He cut her to the quick. "Go, call your husband and come back."

"I have no husband," she replied.

Jesus said to her, "You are right when you say you have no husband. The fact is, you have had five husbands, and the man you now have is not your husband. What you have just said is quite true."

"Sir," the woman said, "I can see that you are a prophet" (John 4:11, 14–19 NIV).

She tried to avoid the subject of her sin, so they jibber-jabbered about worship and mountains and Samaritans for a minute. Then came the kicker.

The woman said, "I know that Messiah (called Christ) is

coming. When he comes, he will explain everything to us."

Then Jesus declared, "I, the one speaking to you—I am he" (John 4:25–26 NIV).

Jesus *never* did that! Jesus never told people He was the Messiah. There is simply not one record of Jesus proclaiming He was the Messiah to a single person. Other people called Him that, but He never announced it Himself. Except to her.

He revealed His saving grace to her—an outcast, a sinner, a divorcée, a woman in sexual sin.

And what did He offer her?

More muddy shame to clog her throat and cloud her eyes and trip her up? A bucket of mud? A boatload of shame? A river of regret?

No. He offered her water that cleansed her heart and filled her evermore: "If you take the water I offer you, you will never be thirsty again."

She believed. She ran and told a bunch of people, and they went and met Him for themselves and begged Him to stay in Samaria for a few more days.

Just the fact that we thirst is proof there is water to drink.

Cleansing must happen inside out. That is why doctors wash the inside of a wound first, before stitching it up.

One day Jesus cried out, "If anyone thirsts, let him come to me and drink. Whoever believes in me, as the Scripture has said, 'Out of his heart will flow rivers of living water.' Now this he said about the Spirit" (John 7:37–39 ESV).

From the living water flowing through the garden of Eden to the book of Revelation, we know that Christ "will guide [us] to springs of living water, and God will wipe away every tear from [our] eyes" (Revelation 7:17 ESV).

This woman knew tears from the eyes. She knew what it felt like to be a broken cistern, holding nothing for long. And

He *knew* her need. He *respected* her longing to be filled. He *understood* the emotional pain, the tears, the heartache. He didn't shame her for it; He offered her an answer.

Thirsty?

One time the Cowboy called me for a date. "Are you thirsty?" he asked.

I was sitting at my desk writing a paper.

"No," I responded. "I'm drinking iced tea."

I didn't realize he was asking me out. I am *that* blond! (My blondness does not come from a bottle. It goes all the way to the root.) He took my no as a denial and tried again the next day.

The Cowboy and I came from two muddy pasts. Before giving our lives back to Christ, our personal pits had turned from mud to quicksand when we were both way too far in to see it happening. Separately, we had both called to Jesus when the muck was swallowing us alive. He had always known the Lord was his friend; I had found the Lord for the first time.

But my darkest cry paled compared to his, so there was grace between us. We became best *friends*. I could be real with him, and he was real with me.

Love is a powerful force—the Song of Songs says that "many waters cannot quench love, neither can floods drown it. . . . Its flashes are flashes of fire the very flame of the Lord" (8:7, 6 ESV).

Love is a fire.

Fires can light whole forests in flames and destroy a lot of property if we aren't guarded by its power.

So we had to contain the fire—as lovers who want sex

to be God's way have to do.

The world says: Use birth control.

God says: Use self-control.

I say: use a fence.

As Proverbs 4:23 (NIV) says, "Above all else, guard your heart, for everything you do flows from it." The heart is the wellspring of life, and when we guard our bodies, we guard our hearts. So we had to keep a strong fence up and keep the gates shut.

As we anticipated our wedding day with a fire that could not be quenched, it was the Holy Spirit who kept us filled. Friends in Christ held us accountable. His Word: our guide. The church: our light. And we streamed to it every Sunday. There we received without cost—the daily bread, the hidden manna, the food of God.

We could not rely on our flesh for self-control. Only the Spirit can give you the power to resist the pull of sex before its time.

Sex does not fill the human soul.

God fills the human soul.

Forgiveness for our pasts made us *pure*, and purity we chose. Our marriage bed has been kissed by God ever since. There have been many times our lives have gotten hard, real hard, and our bed has been a place where we come back to the fire that started it all.

Over the stove in our first home we painted: OUR CUP RUNNETH OVER (see Psalm 23:5 KJV).

For many waters cannot quench love; torrents of rain cannot sweep it away.

Thirsty?

Always.

You will always be thirsty. Men are not designed to fill your cup, as the woman at the well knew. As long as we want men to fill the God-shaped hole in our hearts, we will come up empty. Trying to fill this void with affection or affirmation from people is trying to fill ourselves with water that will surely run out.

We are always thirsty, friend. And there's this offer God makes:

> *"Come, all you who are thirsty, come to the waters; and you who have no money, come, buy and eat! Come, buy wine and milk without money and without cost. Why spend money on what is not bread, and your labor on what does not satisfy? Listen, listen to me, and eat what is good, and you will delight in the richest of fare. Give ear and come to me; listen, that you may live. . . . Seek the LORD while he may be found; call on him while he is near. Let the wicked forsake their ways and their unrighteous thoughts. Let them turn to the LORD, and he will have mercy on him, and to our God, for he will freely pardon them." (Isaiah 55:1–7 NIV)*

Thirsty? Yes. Sign me up to sit by the one who will freely pardon.

Forgiveness

Imagine yourself sitting on the well beside Jesus. He knows everything about you but throws no rocks. Casts no stones. Just offers you an answer to the cries of your heart that no one but Him knows and sees.

If you have not been pure sexually, it is never too late to turn from your ways. It's like the guy who finally puts down the bottle of whiskey and says, "After all of these years, I have to admit, this will never fill me."

Allowing God access not just to your outside life but your inside life cleans you. His water trickles into the places no one sees, washing you from within. The more you allow Him to do this, the more healed you will be.

If you've been in the mud, don't let it stick. He is reaching for you; can you hear His voice? Grab hold of the lifeline that keeps you from sinking in the pit of despair. Hold on to the rope of love and acceptance. He will lift you into a spacious place and offer you water from the well that never runs dry.

MYTH 3:

I Am Stuck with the Shame of My Sin.

(There is no way out of this pit.)

~

TRUTH 3:

You Are Welcome in God's Kingdom,
No Matter Where You've Been.

(He receives you with joy.)

LIFE VERSE:

*No one who hopes in you
will ever be put to shame.*

PSALM 25:3 NIV

Shame Is an Angry Prison Guard

Shame is a double-sided mirror. When pointed at others, shame says, "Shame on *you*!" When pointed at self, shame declares, "Shame on *me*!"

So if you flip the mirror outward and ask, "Shame, shame, who's to blame?" she'll answer, "Everybody else!" But if you flip the mirror toward yourself, shame scowls back at you and says, "You're to blame!" Shame is always turning on you, only presenting two options: blame everyone else or blame yourself.

Shame is a bad friend. She says she'll keep your secrets, even the ones you hide in the dark, but the whole time she keeps your secrets, she's locking you in prison. A furious prison guard, shame cannot be trusted. The longer she keeps you in prison, the more she desires to see you break. Finally, she tells everyone else how shameful you are. You are exposed. You try to blame others, then her, but she keeps pointing the finger back at you.

Then—and this is the worst part—shame tries to follow you around for the rest of your life like a ghost. But this ghost is alive. Sometimes she's really quiet and then sneaks up on you when you aren't looking and sticks out her foot and trips you. You fall flat on your face, bloody and bruised. You try to keep her at bay by letting her ride on your back. You try to be nice to her, but she keeps tricking you. Dangling from her belt loop is the key to your prison, but every time you reach for the key, she disappears into a mist.

When she shows up again, you're wearing her like skin. She is no longer a double-sided mirror or an angry guard or a lurking shadow; she's part of you now. You've become one.

Dealing with Shame

We all have shame of some sort. We mess up a friendship and feel like we can't get it right. We say something we shouldn't and hurt someone we love. We are abused, discarded, rejected. We fear we are not enough: not beautiful enough, not fit enough, not stylish enough, not smart enough, not successful enough. Or we have regrets—and no one can hit the rewind button one time. We don't get a do-over.

No one wants to talk about their shame-filled secret.

And since shame is a lying, cheating, smoke-and-mirrors prison guard, she wants it that way. She doesn't want you to talk about your shame, because if you do—if you are so courageous as to speak your truth: "I feel ashamed about _____"—then it makes it real. Someone will know you cry in the dark, you lock secrets in the closet, you fear, or you sin: you cheat, lie, fail—or someone fails you.

So here's the secret I want to let you in on: we all fail.

We all hear the voice that says, "You are not enough."

Maybe you hear it now.

Maybe you hear it every day.

But the question is, are going to let shame lie to you this way?

Lies rewire your brain into believing they are true. The more you rehearse the same thought, the more it creates a thought pattern in your brain. The more you think *I am not enough*, the more you live out that lie; it will dictate your behavior and poison your relationships.

When we think again and again *I am not _____ enough,* we begin to grasp hold of that thought and allow it to permeate our reality. We believe the lie, then we live it out. Like a marble tipped over a hill of sand, running down the same rivulet again and again, that thought will carve a well-worn pathway in our minds.

It will become our truth.

As a man thinketh in his heart, so is he.[1]

The more you entertain shame's lies about who you are, the more they become your truth, the more you wear shame like skin.

A Beautiful Mirror, a Best Friend

Fear of inadequacy is common to all people, but we must become conquerors over the lies and walk in truth, for the truth will set us free.

Since shame is such a wicked mirror, acting as a never-ending reminder of our failures and flaws, we need a new mirror!

And I have one!

He's a great friend.

He tells you the truth.

He holds the key to your prison.

He is passionate about you, your healing, your freedom.

And He is not a creepy shadow on your back, reminding you of your flaws, or a ghost trying to trip you up.

He actually lights up your path and makes it straight and picks you up when you fall.

He's my best Friend, and I am crazy in love with Him. No, His name isn't Shane. Shane's the Cowboy, and we both know how much I adore him. But in this case I'm talking about the One who wipes Shane's shame good-bye.

I'm talking about (you know who): Jesus.

He's a beautiful mirror: He airbrushes you daily. Now who wouldn't want a friend like that? Jesus is the mirror who reflects compassion and care for you right where you

---

1. See Proverbs 23:7 KJV.

are, even when you are at your worst. Even when there is every reason in the world to give up on you, He will not.

As a mirror, He reflects perfect truth to you every day (even when you have zits, greasy hair, a pudgy belly—and a boatload of mistakes). He speaks back to you in hushed tones of what the Bible calls *agape* love, the highest form of love.

Agape is unconditional love. Agape loves when all other loves quit. Agape cares when there is no reason to care. God "demonstrates His own [agape] love toward us, in that while we were still sinners, Christ died for us" (Romans 5:8 NKJV).

That means that while you were in your sin, He died for you.

God does not look at you through rose-colored glasses, as if you've never failed, hurt yourself, or hurt others. No, He looks at you through the lens of the cross: forgiven. He knows that in your humanity, you are weak; in your fallenness, you need a Savior.

The Story of the Prodigal

God is no double-sided mirror, blaming you and blaming others. He is not a finger pointer. He is the God who said to Adam and Eve, "Don't eat from that tree because it will hurt you."

They did anyway.

He is the God who weeps.

He is the God who says to us, despite our sin, "I have loved you with an everlasting love."[2]

He is the God who summons us home, the One who tells us the story of a prodigal.

In this story, there are two brothers. The younger one asks

---

2. Jeremiah 31:3 NIV

his father for his share of the estate, and the father gives it to him. The boy leaves home and wastes his inheritance on reckless living. He parties it away until he has nothing left.

Then one dark day the boy finds himself feeding pigs to try to make a living, longing to fill his hungry belly with the slop. He is deep in the mud pit when the pain awakens him and alerts him to his senses. He realizes how foolish he has been and rises from the muck, vowing to return to his father and ask for forgiveness.

His father sees him coming a long way off, and compassion fills his tender heart. He runs to his son with open arms, embracing and kissing him.

The son confesses.

The father throws a blanket of shame on him, guilting him for ruining his life.

No! No, no, no! In truth, the father throws a valuable robe around his shoulders, his robe, places a cherished ring on his son's finger, and directs his servants to kill the fattened calf, his prime meat, so they can have a party.

The father does not blame the son for all the partying. The father throws him a party.

Like our heavenly Father, he rejoices that his son is home and exalts in the presence of the one he deeply loves. "My son was dead and is alive! He was lost and is found! Let us eat and celebrate."[3]

The story of the prodigal shows the power of grace to change a life. We are never changed by shame. We are motivated by the *guilt* of knowing how our bad choices hurt us and hurt others, but we are not changed when people guilt us or shame us. The guilt that changes us has to be ours; it has to be our own desire to change for the good.

We are changed when we receive the agape love of

---

3. Luke 15:24, author's paraphrase.

the Father, the unconditional love our hearts are designed to need.

The Cowboy was such a prodigal. The life change he made—the climb to get out of the pit—was propelled by love, for love is the only way out of the life we don't really want.

The Cowboy's Story

Back in the ol' days, there were two lights in hospital waiting rooms: pink and blue.

Men didn't go with their wives into delivery rooms. That space was for the nurses and doctor while the husbands waited.

Back then, when the baby was born, everyone was eager to find out the sex.

So Larry, the Cowboy's father, waited in the waiting room.

The light popped on: Blue! That meant B-O-Y!

"Hallelujah!" Larry said, "I've got a son!"

Shane grew to be the golden boy. Athletic, funny, smart, handsome, and from a wealthy family.

Until he took off, left home, destroyed his life, and crushed his parents' hearts.

Although their son hurt himself and wounded them, they continued to pray he would return home to what he had known as a boy.

One day, Linda's sore mama heart lay bruised before the Lord. Bowed to the ground in a shaft of sunlight, she placed her son's life in God's hands.

And they left the door open.

Seven long years passed.

Then one day, the Cowboy came home. Humbled.

Broken. Sorry. Found.

My son is home! They celebrated. They surrounded him with their agape love and covered him with a blanket of *grace*.

Their cup runneth over, and he drank fresh, clean, living water from the well.

He gave his life back to Christ.

And they keep on celebrating. As long as I have known them—and the Cowboy and I have been married for sixteen years now—they keep on celebrating.

Love

Love doesn't shame us or blame us or cloak us with guilt. "[Love] keeps no record of wrongs."[4] It seems impossible, doesn't it? We want to focus on our faults, our mistakes, our sin record—or hold up the list for someone else for them to see all the ways he or she has offended us.

But love does the impossible, and "what is impossible with man is possible with God" (Luke 18:27 NIV). Love does the unimaginable: love receives us and believes in who we can become regardless of the mud on our faces. Love cloaks us with honor and promises to be faithful to us. Love lavishes us with favor. Love celebrates who we are: sons and daughters of the King of kings, even if we are covered in grime. Love sees who we can be even when we are ugly in plain sight. Love is the greatest gift in all the world, and we are made well when we give and receive a love like this.

Ultimately, we are children of the Most High God—and the sooner we come to our senses and return home to our heavenly Father, the better. He is the God who sees us far

---

4. 1 Corinthians 13:5 NIV

off and comes running with arms open wide, filled to the brim with compassion. He is the Father who sent His Son to die for our sins so that we could be free of shame.

David said, "No one who hopes in you will ever be put to shame" (Psalm 25:3 NIV).

Shame wants us to take the blame. Shame whispers, "Because you did this, you are a loser. You are a whore. You are a murderer. You are a failure. You are not enough. You should be ashamed. God will never forgive you." But Jesus fights back with the cross, and says, "Because you did this, I'll take the penalty."

As Isaiah wrote, "He was pierced for our transgressions. . .crushed for our iniquities; the punishment that brought us peace was on him" (Isaiah 53:5 NIV).

Did you know that on the cross, He *became* your shame? Every ribbon of torn flesh, every spill of warm blood, every striped scar and gaping wound: He took the penalty for our perversion. Why? Why did He do that?

"For the joy set before him he endured the cross, scorning its shame" (Hebrews 12:2 NIV). Do you know that when Jesus was on the cross, the soldiers took all His clothes and divided them up and played a dice game to see who would win His undergarment? Naked, our Maker and Friend hung, beaten and bloodied, mocked and despised, the picture of shame. And He allowed Himself to be crucified for the joy set before Him—the joy of knowing that faith in His blood would bring us entry back home with His heavenly Father, where there is no sin or shame or blame, but only love, joy, hope, and peace—the fulfillment of our hearts' every desire.

As He hung there, He knew that "everything had now been finished" (John 19:28 NIV). His last words were as human as could be: "I am thirsty" (verse 29 NIV).

They gave Him some sour wine. Then "Jesus said, 'It is finished.' With that, he bowed his head and gave up his spirit" (verse 30 NIV).

One sacrifice for all sin, for all humankind. That sin includes your sexual sin. Your abortion, your promiscuity, your sexual immorality, your disease, your robbery, your failure to provide, your failure to protect, and the ways you damaged another's property—their heart and their body. For when He was done, He sat down at the right hand of God.

Christ took the punishment for you. You can now stop blaming yourself and everyone else. You can choose to learn from your mistakes. You can be honest about your pain. You can pursue healing and freedom like it's a race you have to win. But you must not allow shame to follow you around like a shadow on your back, constantly reminding you of your secrets locked in the closet.

Shame need not be your prison guard, for the truth will set you free. The cross is the key to freeing you from shame's power. Take the key. You are shamed no more, because you are loved more than you can ever imagine.

Let that love be a rope for you, right down into the middle of that pit of quicksand.

When you grab it and hold on tight, let Christ wash off all that mud.

Then one day, if someone comes along who needs a rope thrown her way, you'll be the first to toss her a line and help rewrite her story.

MYTH 4:

If I Lock My Secrets Away, I Will Be Okay.

(Don't ask; don't tell.)

—

TRUTH 4:

Walking in the Light Fills You with Light.

(Live by the truth and be set free.)

LIFE VERSE:

If we walk in the light, as he is in the light, we have fellowship with one another, and the blood of Jesus, his Son, purifies us from all sin.

1 JOHN 1:7 NIV

Cutting the Rope

When our pits have turned from mud to quicksand, it feels like there is a rope tied to our ankles, yanking us deeper. The more we pull against the noose looped around our leg, thinking our willpower can break us free, the firmer the grip tightens. The sin seizes us like a snake, yanking us down, and we struggle for air. The sand goes in our mouths and in our eyes, and we can't breathe. We can't see.

This is what sexual sin is like. People say, "Get up and get out!"—and yes, I've said it—you have to get up and get out. But first you must really want to be set free from what has entangled you. You must be *so* determined that instead of yanking on the rope, hoping you can pull yourself away by sheer will, you cut the rope. Not because I'm telling you to, but because you want freedom like you want air. You want that key out of your prison, and you want to see light. You must *want* light like you *want* life to chase yourself out of the darkness.

And if *you* want it—not your mother or friend or brother—Y-O-U—then you must cut all ties with the thing that is hurting you and your future, and you must put barriers around your heart, and I'm going to tell you how to do that. But first, know this: none of us can get away without breaking free from the noose tied to our leg. To do that, we need help. We need to say out loud, "There's a rope wrapped around my leg, and I need help cutting it off!"[1]

A lot of people say they want to be set free from their past, but they don't cut the rope. They stay steeped in the mud. Whether the sin is sexual immorality, adultery, or pornography, they try to keep it in the dark, deny it's there, and still hope to break free.

Not possible.

1. Ted Roberts, *Pure Desire* (Minneapolis: Bethany House, 2008), 43–52.

As long as you are steeped in sin, pain, addiction, or self-harm of any sort and yet keep saying, "I'm fine, I'm fine," the noose gets tighter, the grip carves into your ankle, the quicksand sucks you in, and you get so deep you'd just as soon drown in it. The pit destroys hope, demolishes futures—but God is the giver of hope and a future.[2] He desires to protect the sexuality of His people so they can live abundant lives free of shame and regret. His design for marriage is for sex to be wonderful with the person you love for the rest of your life. That is His desire, His purpose for sex.

But the enemy wants to "steal and kill and destroy" (John 10:10 NLT) and he works tirelessly to rob us of the abundant life that lies within the borders of God's blessing.

The slow, sinking loss often begins with a very slight opening into your sexuality when you are young, and the opening grows and grows. It grows the more you give yourself away and the more it is taken from you, and eventually it ends in sinking hopelessness—this breathlessness, this numbness, this pain that none of us wants to know.

I know because I'm a girl who struggled, a girl who sank, a girl who can still remember the noose around the leg. I cut the rope. I broke free. I grabbed hold of the lifeline tethered by the King of grace, and His arm lifted me out of the quicksand and led me to a bank of light.

Tugging against the rope was like denying it was there, and the more we deny it's there, the firmer its grip. But one day we come to our senses. We admit: "I need up and out. I need help." We cut the rope. We leave everything behind. Like the prodigal son, we speak our truth in the light. And we walk into our futures.

The future is paved with light. For God's Word is "a lamp

2. Jeremiah 29:11

to my feet and a light to my path" (Psalm 119:105 NASB).

The Word says that God preserves both man and beast, that His faithful love is so valuable that people take refuge in the shadow of His wings. We are filled from the abundance of His house; He lets us drink from His refreshing stream, for with Him is life's fountain. In His light we will see light.[3]

It takes courage to cut the rope—to grab onto the tether of grace and accept the offer to be pulled up and out, to allow God to place you in an expanse of light. This is the offer I'm making to you now. Grab hold. Let your body go loose, but keep a firm grip on the rope that is pulling you out. Cut the tether to the pit, and rise.

The Light

At first, if you've been in the quicksand, basking in the light feels warm. It feels good on your shoulders and radiates on your face. The feeling of sun on your skin is delicious to all the senses.

The light of Christ coming into our dark places begins to fill us. If our souls are like caves that long to be filled, His light illuminates the cave and shines into the corners of our souls. This is good! This is beautiful.

As we are lit from within, however, we may find yucky things hanging out in the shadows of our souls. The light illuminates everything—the good, the bad, the ugly. Grime, muck, mire—residue from our sin or those sins committed against us—that ache, that heartbreak, that dismissal of our value that we experienced in the dark or even on the road with God. Just because you are a Christian does not

---

3. Psalm 36:7–9

mean you don't hurt. Of course you do. You hurt. Someone tripped you, said something that pained you, and it drove a road into the corner of your soul and parked there. Maybe the wound set up shop and started operating within you, like a corner store. Actions came from your woundedness, but those actions were death to you. Maybe you've been in habitual sin for so long that you have a whole row of shops set up and operating in your life that you need to break down, sort through, and move on out!

So here you are now, in Christ, and His light has come into your soul. It feels good; it feels great. But His light also shines on the things that are not good.

The lies we believe that start like this: "I am not enough. . . ."

The myths we've bought into, like "I can play in the mud and not get muddy."

The operations doing business in our souls that hurt us and hurt others.

The hiding.

The lying about it.

The pretending it's not there.

The falling back into the pit over and over because we thought our willpower would keep us out.

People often think hiding their sin is the best thing to do. In other words, "Don't ask; don't tell. Let's pretend like everything is perfect even though it's not." If young people knew they could go to their parents and openly talk about sexual experiences and feelings—being absolutely sure they wouldn't be met with shame and anger—they would do it more often.

The Cowboy read a book once called *Raising Cole.*[4] In

---

4. Mark Pittman, *Raising Cole: Developing Life's Greatest Relationship, Embracing Life's Greatest Tragedy: A Father's Story* (HCI, 2004).

the book, the dad taught his son he could talk to him about anything under the sun, and he wouldn't get in trouble as long as they labeled the conversation "Dead Man's Talk." So, in our family, we have adopted "Dead Man's Talk." In other words: if you ask me to, I'll act like a "dead man," and you can tell me anything you want and I'm just going to listen. I'm not going to punish, shame, or get angry at you; I'm also not going to repeat anything you tell me. If you want me to. . .and if need be, I'll give you some advice or get you some help, but you can come to me about anything, free from shame.

Whether you can have "Dead Man's Talk" with a counselor, friend, mentor, parent, or even with the Lord, then you have found a safe place where you can be real, open, honest, and unashamed.

But if you keep your shame hidden, you invite shadows to haunt you. Such is the story of Tamar.

Tamar's Shame

There is a story in the Bible about a girl who was raped. Her name is Tamar. It is her half-brother who violates her, and when her other brother hears of it, he tells her to keep it quiet, to not "take it to heart."

"Don't speak of it, my sister," were the words Tamar's brother spoke. In other words, pretend like it never happened. Take that evil violation of your tender sexuality and bury it in the back corner of your soul. Spend the rest of your life acting as if it doesn't live there.

When it happened, Tamar had begged her half-brother not to rape her, and her plea echoes in the blackness of eternity: "Don't do this horrible thing! As for me, where would I carry my shame?" (2 Samuel 13:12–13).

The answer? Hold it in, sister, hold it in—and when it burned in her brother like a fiery furnace, he avenged the rape of Tamar by murdering the one who violated her. When truth wants to burst forth like an angry strike of lightning, the answer for so many girls is: Don't tell. Keep silent. Hide it.

Because if a girl said it out loud—"It exists! It happened! He did that to me, that wicked thing. Or worse, maybe I let it happen!" . . . Oh, how she would be stuck with the shame.

The last we hear of Tamar is: She lived a desolate woman.[5]

The Word of God says of rape: "Women are raped in Zion, young women in the towns of Judah. . .for this our heart has become sick, for this our eyes have grown dim."[6]

If she spoke of the wicked act, if she said it out loud, how outrageous it was, the way she was humiliated. . .she'd be the one wearing the stained rags, right? Admit it to be true: if a girl doesn't fight for herself in this world, if she is not protected, she is the one disgraced. She is the one branded.

How odd Tamar, the daughter of King David—was branded by her half-brother's sin, motivated by lust. . .an act so vile and ugly. . .and even her own father didn't convict him for it.

But that's the way the world goes for girls sometimes—a man lusts after her and acts on it, but she is branded. It's not right, but it's often true.

I read a book called *Lucky* once.[7] In this memoir, the girl was violently raped and beaten, but she survived. Everyone told her she was "lucky" she lived. *Lucky?* . . .

---

5. 2 Samuel 13:20.

6. Lamentations 5:17.

7. Alice Sebold, *Lucky* (Back Bay Books, 2002).

she cried in her book. *Really?*

What is funny, but not funny at all, is Tamar's half-brother took advantage of her because she was beautiful. But Tamar is the one who ended up living with the disgrace. She was the one who tore her precious robe. She was the one who smeared ash on her face. She was the one who lived desolate.[8] Her virginity was torn, her purity robbed; shame was the makeup she wore. She never married, bore children, or lived out her destiny as the beloved daughter of the king, the one named after God's own heart. Driven by lust, her half-brother violated her; consumed with wrath, her real brother avenged her; and her father was set free through forgiveness.[9] But Tamar lived shackled.

Why?

Because shame is an angry prison guard.

Shame is a shadow, steeping us in darkness.

And we keep her there for fear of what would happen if truth came to light.

But we can choose a better road: lit.

Healing

Hiding your hurt is the worst thing you can do. It is better to talk about it, to put it in the light. Allowing God to shine His light into your dark places is the beginning of being set free from them. His light will shine in the far corners of the cave within you and illuminate the ugly—lighting up the operations taking place in your life that are detrimental to you now. Maybe you were a victim once, but that doesn't mean you need to remain a victim your whole life. God can give you victory over sin and victory over your past—this is true.

8. 2 Samuel 13:20
9. 2 Samuel 14:33

The devil's way is to steal what is rightfully God's. Our sexuality is set apart for marriage—this is clear as day. The devil gains entry through our minds, convincing us we will get the love we need through sex. But he is a liar. When he enters into the mind of a young girl or boy, he takes up residence and splashes images in their minds. For boys, they are often images that ignite sexual arousal. For girls, they are often images of our painful pasts—since we were never designed to be used like things for the pleasure of boys, or even for our pleasure. Pleasure is a gift from God—it is not a bad thing at all! But sexual pleasure outside the safety of marriage leads to consequences we'd rather live without.

Our bodies were designed to nurture our husbands, to be the soft landing after their hard day, to ease the anguish of the wars they fight in the world. We were designed to help and support men with the nurture only a woman can provide. Our bodies are designed to bear children, to nurse babies and love families. We are created to be complements and helpers to the men at our side. Our bodies are to be the object of our husband's desire only.

Our bodies are beautiful gifts to our husbands—the feminine beauty a glorious treasure of luscious, sweet tenderness next to our male counterparts, whose strength is fierce and mighty, strong as a bull.

But your man will want all of you. He will not settle for less—and if he does, he is missing out.

If and when you do get married, you want to be shame-free and whole. You'll want to give your husband and family everything you've got, and you won't want to be shackled by regret from the past or secrets of the present. So do the courageous work to heal and get free. Sometimes we have to face the ugly so we can get to beautiful.

The Counselor

Shame is a double-sided mirror, both accusing us and blaming others. But God is a crystal clear mirror. He helps us see ourselves and our own responsibility clearly, challenging us to be better versions of ourselves and releasing our shame by His grace. Shame is an angry prison guard, hiding the key by convincing us to keep our secrets in the darkness where they cannot be seen. But the Spirit of God is our Counselor. The prophet Isaiah said of Jesus: "and his name shall be called Wonderful Counselor, Mighty God, Everlasting Father, Prince of Peace" (Isaiah 9:6 ESV).

In predicting His own death just as Isaiah had, Jesus promised that after He died, He would not leave us alone. He promised us a Counselor, "the Spirit of truth. . .[who] will guide you into all the truth" (John 16:13 ESV).

To walk in the light, you must find a safe place to talk. Talking openly in the light with a counselor who is trained in biblical truth is a powerful and transformative experience. This is not something you do randomly without commitment.

Revisiting the past is not fun, but it does help us sort the good from the bad. We are to "test everything. . . . Hold on to what is good" (1 Thessalonians 5:21). So go through the heart-wrenching process of testing everything. Looking at everything. Your whole story in all its parts and pieces.

Like sifting pearls from sand, we have to sift through the blame, shame, and anger and hold on to the good parts of our stories. Pour out the bowl of your pain at the feet of the

Lord and say, "Take it. I don't want to carry this forever." It may take a lot of time. Years even.

Get open and stop hiding. As Jesus says, "There is nothing concealed that will not be revealed, or hidden that will not be known. What I tell you in the darkness, speak in the light" (Matthew 10:26–27 NASB). In this passage, Jesus compares us to a sparrow. He says, "Do not fear" and tells us that even a little bird doesn't fall to the ground without Him knowing about it. "The very hairs of your head are all numbered. So do not fear; you are more valuable than many sparrows" (Matthew 10:28, 30–31).

In other words, He knows. When you fall, He sees it. When you feel naked and bare, kicking about in your blood, He passes by.[10]

So you *can* talk about it. You *can.* Because He already knows. You are never alone.

> *This is the message we have heard from him and declare to you: God is light; in him there is no darkness at all. If we claim to have fellowship with him and yet walk in the darkness, we lie and do not live out the truth. But if we walk in the light, as he is in the light, we have fellowship with one another, and the blood of Jesus, his Son, purifies us from all sin. (1 John 1:5–7 NIV)*

The cross is the only solution—His blood can wash you white as snow. Then there will be no traces of your shame left written on the tender parchment paper of your heart.

He "forgave all our sins. He canceled the record of the charges against us and took it away by nailing it to the cross" (Colossians 2:13–14).

---

10. Ezekiel 16:6

Whatever the marks of shame written on your heart—if you bring them to the cross, the handwriting vanishes.

There is no record of your sin.

You are flawless, a transparent cloth—so clean, so pure, that your soul appears never to have been written on at all.

Such is the soul who has laid her heart at Jesus' feet. You who have overcome such sin, He will give you a white robe to wear and a white stone with a new name written on it.

I wonder what your new name will be:

Never Abandoned. Accompanied. Bride. Perfect. Chosen. Redeemed. Beloved. Evergreen. Radiant. Washed. Silver and Sparkling Clean, a Jewel. Rock of Strength. Faithful. Beautiful in My Eyes. Joy. Hope. Together with Christ, Forever Married. Living Water, the One Whose Cup Overflows.

You choose: what do you want your new name to be?

MYTH 5:

It's My Body, and I Get to Choose!

(What I do with it is my business, lady.)

——

TRUTH 5:

It's Not Your Body, but You Do Get to Choose.

(Your body is not your own; you were bought at a price.)

LIFE VERSE:

Do you not know that your bodies are temples of the Holy Spirit, who is in you, whom you have received from God? You are not your own; you were bought at a price.

1 CORINTHIANS 6:19–20 NIV

Where the Glory Dwells

Your body is like a house for your spirit. When you die, that house will dissolve to dust, just as wood decomposes and combines with the earth again. You came from dust, and to dust you shall return. But your spirit lives forever. In heaven you will be given a glorified body, the embodiment of perfection and virtue. There will be no lack, no sin, no pain, no loss; all will be complete. You will be filled with an inexpressible and glorious joy.

It used to be that people had to go to a physical building to encounter the presence of God. But that's no longer the case. Since the death, burial, and resurrection of Jesus, the Holy Spirit, the Spirit of Jesus Christ, takes up residence in your body. When you ask Him to be the Lord of your life, His Spirit enters in and lives within you; you become a vessel for Christ. Your body is the temple of the Holy Spirit—He lives and moves and acts from within you. It's a beautiful thing when you really grasp it.

Living in your body like it's God's house instead of your possession changes the way you think about your body.

We wouldn't stand by and watch as robbers broke into the church and stole from it. We would fight to protect the house of God. We would mark it off as holy ground—not like the abandoned building down the street. We would not allow God's house to become dilapidated or degraded, and we wouldn't stand by and applaud while people committed heinous crimes within its walls.

We take care of God's house because it's the place His glory dwells—and if you are in Christ, you are God's house. You are the temple, the place He lives and moves and has His being.[1]

---

1. Acts 17:28

You Choose

How you take care of the house for your spirit is your choice. No one but you is responsible for the care and keeping of your temple. No matter how hard you try, you will not find anyone else who wants to take full responsibility for caring for *your* healthy body. Hands down, it's up to *you* to exercise, get plenty of rest, eat right, and take care of the house for your spirit. It's up to *you* to dress well, apply makeup, and do your hair to highlight your best features. (FYI: I'm writing this while wearing my favorite old, tattered jeans, and my hair is begging to be washed—but my plan is to go running later and wash my hair and shave for my husband tonight. I swear I will!) Bottom line, we are not designed to look perfect and be perfect, but it's our responsibility to care for our bodies, dress with dignity and style, and reflect goodness and grace—these are things that we can choose, but we have to pick them.

We can either preserve or pollute our temples. Life presents us with the choice not to exercise, to eat trashy food, to gorge and be lazy, to dress ourselves in unflattering clothes, or even to apply way too much makeup so people focus on the makeup instead of us. We get to pick! We can fill our bodies with drugs and alcohol and hand out sexual favors to whomever we please—or we can protect our sexuality as something precious to be enjoyed in marriage. We pick; we choose.

Listen to the sound of God's voice offering you choices: "I have set before you life and death, blessing and curse. Therefore choose life, that you and your offspring may live" (Deuteronomy 30:19 ESV).

In my life, I have chosen wrong and right. I have chosen death and life. I am aware of the consequences of both choices. When we choose life, there are blessings; when we choose death, there are curses. Sex can open wide the door for either route.

So we *have the choice* to offer up our bodies and minds in sexual immorality. If we make that choice, there will be consequences, as there are to every choice, good or bad.

Before the Womb I Knew You

By the laws of our land, we have the legal choice to terminate the life of a child in our own womb. This can be done whether or not the father agrees with the decision. In some states, teens need parental approval to have an abortion; in other states they do not.[2] In this country, teen girls can get an abortion before they are legally allowed to take a sip of wine or cast their vote for mayor. But in no state does the father have legal rights to protect the life of his child while he or she is still in the womb.

Regardless of what the law says, the laws of God are supreme. He is a "father to the fatherless" (Psalm 68:5). So even if there is no earthly father present to mold and shape the life of the child, the heavenly Father is forming and shaping that life. As Isaiah puts it, "But now, O LORD, you are our Father; we are the clay and you are our potter; we are all the work of your hand" (Isaiah 64:8 ESV). He forms our inward parts and knits us together in our mother's womb. A child's frame is not hidden from Him when she is intricately woven in the secret place; even there His eyes see her unformed body. His works are wonderful. . .and we

---

2. For more information, see optionline.org and ramahinternational.org.

know that full well.[3]

We are made in the image of God,[4] and God is the Creator of life. Our worth is something that no man can create and no man can destroy.

> *Thus says the L*ORD*, your Redeemer, who formed you from the womb: "I am the L*ORD*, who made all things, who alone stretched out the heavens, who spread out the earth by myself. . .who says. . .'He is my shepherd, and he shall fulfill all my purpose.' " (Isaiah 44:24–28 ESV)*

The same word God uses to "form" us is the same word He uses to form the earth: "For behold, he who *forms* the mountains and creates the wind. . .who. . .treads on the heights of the earth—the LORD, the God of hosts, is his name!" (Amos 4:13 ESV).

Scripture teaches that He knew us even *before the womb.* As He said to Jeremiah: "Before I formed you in the womb I knew you, and before you were born I consecrated you; I appointed you a prophet to the nations" (Jeremiah 1:5 ESV). We are given identity, value, and purpose *before* the womb and *before* we are born. Every single one of us was known by God before the moment of conception, and He destined a purpose for our lives. We are woven as a tapestry in the womb—and He writes our destiny. "All the days ordained for me were written in your book before one of them came to be" (Psalm 139:16 NIV). In other words, He knew your story before He wrote it.

In a strange way, I understand this. I lived my story before I wrote it. My first book, *Girl Perfect*, was written long after the story had unfolded. So it is with our stories: God is timeless. He knew you before you were born; your days were destined by Him; and your life and purpose are

---

3. Psalm 139:13–16
4. Genesis 1:26–27

eternal. These are things no man can give to you and no man can take away.

Therefore, nothing that man does to destroy life in the womb can eliminate the spirit or purpose of that child.

People killed God's one and only Son, but that did not end Jesus' life or legacy. The termination of a pregnancy does not end that child's story. People may kill the body, but they cannot kill the soul.

It's a funny thing that people ask the question: When does life begin? At the moment of conception? At twelve weeks? Twenty-four? Thirty-six? The moment of birth? Yet who asks the Creator of life?

His Word is clear as day. We are born in Him before we are born on earth. See what He says to His people:

> "[You] who have been borne by me from before your birth, carried from the womb; even to your old age I am he, and to gray hairs I will carry you. I have made, and I will bear; I will carry and will save. . . . For I am God, and there is no other; I am God, and there is none like me, declaring the end from the beginning. . .saying, 'My counsel shall stand, and I will accomplish my purpose'. . . . I have spoken, and I will bring it to pass; I have purposed, and I will do it." (Isaiah 46:3–4, 9–11 ESV)

Sometimes we make rules for ourselves. As humans, we try to decide what is right and wrong, what is true and what isn't. But it is easier to understand who we are in light of who God is. Our "Maker" is His name.[5] We are His "workmanship [his craftsmanship], created in Christ Jesus for good works, which God prepared beforehand" (Ephesians 2:10 ESV).

---

5. Isaiah 17:7; 51:13

Children who were aborted in this life are running and giggling in the throes of heaven now. Nothing man does to destroy human life can take away the purpose of God.

For the thief comes to "steal and kill and destroy," but Jesus came that we "may have life and have it abundantly" (John 10:10 ESV).

Dan's Story

When I asked women to write to me about their abortion stories for this book, I didn't expect one to come from a man. Dan is a father of five: he has four children on earth and one in heaven. He is the baseball coach to his three sons and his only daughter's steady date to her tea parties. There is no greater joy for him than being a daddy. When his children were babies, they slept in his big, strong arms; and as they grew, he taught them to be powerful and true to their family name.

But there was a time when Dan was young and dumb, before he met his faithful wife-to-be. During college, he fell for a girl named Cindy.

Dan was raised in a family with traditional values but had turned his heart to partying when Cindy became pregnant. Unplanned and unexpected, this pregnancy rattled their little worlds. Together in the doctor's office, they viewed the ultrasound of their baby growing in her womb, and Dan tucked the black-and-white picture in his shirt pocket.

He took Cindy home to see his parents, and together they told them they were going to have a baby. Dan gave his mother the picture of the ultrasound, and she tacked it on her refrigerator. They knew Cindy was not the best for him, but they accepted the truth of this new life, and so did Dan.

He made the decision to marry her and raise his child—to "do the right thing," not because she was the "right girl" or it was the "right circumstance," but because he knew it was the honorable thing to do.

His newfound purpose of becoming a father inspired him to clean up his life and get his act together. For the first time in a long time, Dan saw through the broken glass a glimmer of hope. Through this new life, he found purpose. He actually became excited about becoming a father.

Dan returned to work so he could support his new family. Then one day he came home and Cindy's aunt and she were sitting on the couch, Cindy's face as white as a ghost. She needn't say a word. He knew.

"What have you done?" he cried.

What he knew was true. She had gotten an abortion.

Dan exploded in a fury.

"You killed our baby?" he screamed. "You destroyed my own flesh and blood without even talking to me about it! How could you? How could you?"

The treasure of the sonogram picture flashed across his mind. Was it to be a girl or boy?

He began throwing things and crashing furniture to the ground. In a moment of utter desperation, he grabbed a kitchen knife and sliced his own wrist. "You want to sacrifice me? Is my blood not enough?" he cried.

The cut went much deeper than he expected, and he was bleeding profusely.

"I love you! I love you!" she cried.

The hospital bandaged his wounds, but Dan was deeply scarred. Waking in a fury of righteous indignation, the next day he went straight to the place where she had the abortion. He walked up to the counter and screamed at them for helping a girl kill his child without his consent.

"It takes two, lady!" he seethed. "You allowed this girl to come in here and make a decision that is not hers to make alone. It takes two to make a baby, and that involves *me*! That was my baby, my kid! This involves us both! If she were to have that baby, I would raise that kid! The law would make me support my kid, right? But you have stolen him from me—or her—I don't even know—but God knows! Shame on you for even working in a place like this! I hope you go to hell for doing this to people!"

As you may imagine, he was escorted out of the abortion clinic.

But his cries would not be drowned out. Never has he hated someone the way he hated Cindy—and for her aunt, there were no words. He tried to drink away his sorrow.

But his pain only skyrocketed. When he returned to the apartment and saw her again, Dan crushed vases, broke lamps, turned over tables. Cindy called the police. He was arrested and put in prison for four months for destruction of property.

Just as Dan knew the southern plains of Georgia where he was raised—the traditions, the truths, the Sundays of rest—Dan knew the laws and ordinances of God. What is more, he knew the heart of the Father—and that Spirit lived in him even when he was not living his best life. He was a beautiful mess, not unlike Jesus who went into the temple and flipped over the tables, spilling everything everywhere and knocking out the lies, driving out the filth from God's holy place—with the Holy Spirit living in his heart, Dan knew how to clear a temple of sin.

But the crime committed against him broke his heart. And from that broken place forged a fiery bolt of anger that still smoldered later in life. He often feared something would happen to his four precious children, his blessed wife, and wondered why his anger flashed so easily.

Dan will tell you: it's not just your body, your choice; daddies have a say too. Fathers matter.

Our country doesn't recognize the father's right to his child until after that child is born. After the baby is born, he bears the legal responsibility to support his child; but while the baby is in the womb, he has no legal rights. Therefore, we have millions of daddies in our country grappling with the termination of their children in the womb through abortion, a decision over which many of them had no say.

***

My Body, My Choice

The culture's lie is: "It's my body, and what I do with it is my business!" But the truth is: It's God's body; He made it, and He bought it for a price on the cross. Therefore, we are to honor God with our bodies. Our bodies are the temples of the Holy Spirit, the place His glory dwells.

So it's not your body. But you do get to choose how you live in it. And your choices don't just affect you. They affect your family and those who love you. Ultimately, they will affect your future.

So choose wisely.

MYTH 6:

A Baby Is a Burden.

(And this is not a convenient time to be pregnant. . .)

—

TRUTH 6:

A Baby Is a Blessing.

(So give the gift of life.)

LIFE VERSE:

*Children are a gift from the LORD;
they are a reward from him.*
PSALM 127:3 NLT

Make Your Plans in Pencil

Our daughter is futuristic. She dreams about the future, makes plans, and fully expects those dreams to come true. But when the Cowboy listens to her elaborate visions of a near-perfect future, he will often peer over his reading glasses—looking so darn handsome—and say to her, "Always make your plans in pencil, sweetheart."

He knows. You make your plans, but the Lord writes your story.

Boo's Story

In researching this book, I asked my Facebook friends to send me their stories. My first request was for abortion stories, and I received one from a courageous woman named Boo, who told me about the flip side of abortion: adoption. The power of this story is enough to change any heart. Although her story is in third person, they are her words, not mine:

On April 27, 1970, Boo was born. Her birth mother chose to give her life, and in a brave and unselfish act of love, she placed her for adoption. Boo's parents never tried to hide the fact that she was adopted. From the time she was a child, they told her she was specially chosen for their family and how precious she was because of that. Not only did God give her wonderful parents, but He also gave her three older brothers.

Fast forward to when she was fifteen. One night at a friend's party, Boo gave herself away sexually to a boy that she barely knew. She did it mainly to fit in because "all her friends were doing it." It wasn't how she expected her first time to be, not at all like the romance we see on TV and in movies. A couple of days later, the boy moved away to live with his dad. She never saw or heard from him again.

Boo began feeling guilty and shameful, but that only made her think that she could never go back and start over. So, about five months later, she found herself in another sexual relationship. As the days went by, she sank deeper into a pit. The question rang in her ears, *How in the world could I do this, especially to my family?* Her parents and brothers had no idea; they saw her as their "perfect" little girl.

Then one night Boo thought the only way out of the mess was to take her life. She found a bottle of pain pills and took them. The phone rang; it was the guy she was seeing, and she told him what she had done. He hung up the phone, and the next thing she knew her parents were there and she was in the emergency room.

After being given ipecac to make her vomit and asked several questions, the hospital gave her a pregnancy test: it came back positive. Her secret was out. Not knowing what to do, her parents called their pastor. They discussed it with him and decided an abortion was the route to go. The next day her parents made the appointment, and they were on their way to the nearest town that did abortions.

When the clinician called her number, Boo was taken to a room where the doctor did an ultrasound to see where the "blob of tissue" was (that's what abortion clinics call forming babies). He asked her the date of her last period, and she told him it was just a couple weeks before.

"Are you sure?" he asked, and she said she was. Suddenly he stopped the ultrasound and said, "You are twenty-eight weeks pregnant. . .too far along to have an abortion."

The lightbulb went on, and Boo realized she got pregnant the first time she had sex. The drive home seemed like an eternity.

While she lay down in the backseat of the car, she made

the choice to place her baby for adoption. Her parents got in touch with an adoption agency and got the ball rolling. Boo had about a month before school was out for summer. No one knew she was pregnant, not even her best friend. She only gained twelve pounds and had her period the whole time.

On July 16, 1986, Boo gave birth to the most beautiful baby boy. She got to hold him, feed him, change his diapers, and tell him that she loved him. She wanted him to understand how much she loved him and wanted the best for him. She went back to school that fall.

In her words, "The walls were up. . .the locks were locked. . .the key was thrown away. I didn't talk about it, and neither did my family."

During the next seven years, Boo stuffed her pain and continued to have other sexual relationships. Within that time she also got married, but it ended in divorce two years later. Then she began adding alcohol to the mix, going to clubs, going home with strangers. . . "It. Was. Awful. I was a complete wreck," Boo describes.

Then one night Boo met a guy on a blind date. A year later they got married, and the early years were "disastrous, to say the least." They fought, drank, partied, and "thought only of themselves." But they were "living it up," so they thought they had the life! They believed if they had a baby that would fill the void.

After two years of trying with no success, Boo began asking God why He was punishing her. *Doesn't He want me to be happy?* she wondered. *Is this because I placed my baby for adoption?* Deeper and deeper she sank.

But. . .God!

Boo and her husband began attending church. Between partying, putting themselves first, and trying to get pregnant, something began happening to them. Bit by bit their hearts were breaking, and their view of God was changing.

Then one day God spoke directly to Boo's heart and said He wanted her for His own. The same exact thing happened with her husband.

In Boo's words, "God in His great mercy saved me (us) and forgave me (us). . .and because of the blood of Jesus I was free! Free from the guilt. . . I was a new creation!" She and her husband were baptized together on September 1, 2002, and they began to put God first.

Scarred but Set Free

Boo and her husband, Mike, still longed for a child but soon discovered that Boo had extensive scarring on her fallopian tubes and ovaries—caused by an STD called chlamydia, which can cause infertility in women if left untreated. Boo never even knew she had contracted an STD—she had no symptoms—and if chlamydia is unchecked, it can cause permanent damage.

In Boo's words: "The choice to have sex outside of God's boundaries of marriage literally scarred me for life."

She had extensive surgery to clean up the scarring, and after *eight years of trying,* she became pregnant! She was overjoyed.

But sadly, it was an ectopic pregnancy, which means the baby was forming in the fallopian tube instead of the uterus. The baby could not survive, and it was life-threatening for Boo, so she lost the baby. Then, she had another pregnancy, and there was even a heartbeat! But that baby died as well because it was developing in the fallopian tube. At that time, she faced a double whammy: the chlamydia had damaged her reproductive system so much she could not have a baby.

Yet Boo believed God was right there with her, and He was going to walk them down this path.

One day, a young lady from church approached Boo. She had heard Boo's adoption story and was pregnant and wanted to place her baby for adoption. She knew in her heart that she was carrying someone else's blessing but didn't know where to begin. Boo shared about their walk down the road of infertility, the two precious babies they had lost, and how God impressed on their hearts to sit still, keep praying, and expect Him to answer in His time.

At that moment, the girl looked at Boo with tears streaming down her face and said, "You and Mike are the answer to my prayers."

Mike and Boo Seller's son was born on March 29, 2008. Boo even got to be in the delivery room, and she still attends church with the birth mother's family.

She ended her letter to me this way:

> Every day I get to enjoy life because my birth mama chose life and placed me for adoption. Every day I get to enjoy knowing that in God's mercy, kindness, and grace He allowed me to give life and place my baby for adoption. . . . Every day my husband and I get to spend time with the cutest redhead who totally, completely, without a doubt loves life to the fullest all because his birth mama chose life and allowed us to adopt him. . . . God takes everything and makes it beautiful in His time. . . In Jesus, you are flawless.

> — *Boo Sellers*

Choose Life

If at this moment in time, or at any time in the future, you find yourself facing an unplanned pregnancy, be *strong*. Be *brave*. Take *courage*. You are not alone, and you may just be carrying someone else's heart's cry—someone else's blessing.

Speak up and tell someone who can help you—don't run to an abortion clinic. Run to someone who knows the Lord and His dreams for life. And if someone disagrees with your choices—or if lots of people do, even your own parents—well then, you have the authority as God's chosen and beloved daughter to stand up and say: "I'm choosing life. God knew this child from before the womb. He is forming a life within me; and I will honor Him in this."

No matter what the culture says, you can take heart by clinging to these truths:

♡ *"Children are a gift from the LORD; they are a reward from Him."*

♡ *"Children born to a young man are like arrows in a warrior's hands."*

♡ *"Those who fear the LORD are secure; he will be a refuge for their children."*[1]

Sex makes babies; yes, it's true. What's also true is that a baby is a blessing. So we can rest assured that God will be a fortress for your children, whether they are planned or unplanned. Being a parent is incredibly hard work; it requires sacrificial love that is neither convenient nor easy. But it is a privilege to cocreate with God to shape a life, and the decision must never be done halfheartedly.

So if you choose life and choose to raise a child, then

1. Psalm 127:3; Psalm 127:4; Proverbs 14:26

you do it with all the strength God supplies, and there is no end to His provision.

And if you chose abortion at any point in your journey, that child is with God. Know that He redeems everything lost in the womb and outside of it. His specialty is to bring blessing from cursing, life from death, purpose from pain. "Behold, children are a heritage from the LORD, the fruit of the womb a reward" (Psalm 127:3 ESV). Notice the period at the end of that sentence. No matter how a child comes into the world and how that child leaves the world, the life of that child is eternal. Whether in heaven or on earth, the destiny of that child may surprise us. Whether dancing in the throes of heaven or walking the dirt of earth, our children may impact the world in far greater ways than we ever will.

MYTH 7:

I Plan My Pregnancies.

(And my future.)

—

TRUTH 7:

God Controls the Womb.

(Peace comes through trust.)

LIFE VERSE:

*God blessed them and said to them,
"Be fruitful and increase in number;
fill the earth and subdue it."*

GENESIS 1:28 NIV

Plans Written in Red

So there are your plans, written in pencil; and then, there are the red letters. Red-letter Bibles are my favorite. We can flip open the pages and Jesus' words shine like lights sparkling on the mantel, highlighting truth for where we are right now, at this moment—and what we need to know.

Just because a girl saves sex for marriage doesn't mean it's all going to come out picture perfect—we're not making that promise here. It simply means she chose to honor God with her body before marriage, which is going to make her a lot more likely to honor God's work in her body after marriage. Who we are before marriage carries over to who we become.

Mary, the mother of Jesus, must have had plans for her engagement and coming wedding to Joseph when the angel Gabriel stopped her in her tracks.

> *"Greetings, O favored one, the Lord is with you!" the angel said. But she was greatly troubled at the saying, and tried to discern what sort of greeting this might be. (It's not every day an angel speaks to you.)*
>
> *The angel said to her, "Do not be afraid, Mary, for you have found favor with God. And behold, you will conceive in your womb and bear a son, and you shall call his name Jesus. He will be great and will be called the Son of the Most High. And the Lord God will give to him the throne of his father David, and he will reign over the house of Jacob forever, and of his kingdom there will be no end."*

(*Right*, Mary must be thinking, *and I am a teenager!*)

> *Mary said to the angel, "How will this be, since I am a virgin?"*
>
> *And the angel answered her, "The Holy Spirit will come upon you, and the power of the Most*

High will overshadow you; therefore the child to be born will be called holy—the Son of God. And behold, your relative Elizabeth in her old age has also conceived a son, and this is the sixth month with her who was called barren. For nothing will be impossible with God."

And Mary said, "Behold, I am the servant of the Lord; let it be to me according to your word." And the angel departed from her.[1]

Let's get this straight. Mary was a virgin, engaged to be married, and Elizabeth was old and barren, which means she believed she couldn't have a child. Yet the angel's words rang true: Mary miraculously became pregnant with and birthed the Messiah, and Elizabeth bore the one who would prepare the road for Jesus, John the Baptist.

Mary had no choice but to erase all her plans, including what people thought of her, and write new ones to prepare for the coming Christ child.

And her husband Joseph, being a just man and unwilling to put her to shame, resolved to divorce her quietly. But as he considered these things, behold, an angel of the Lord appeared to him in a dream, saying, "Joseph, son of David, do not fear to take Mary as your wife, for that which is conceived in her is from the Holy Spirit. She will bear a son, and you shall call his name Jesus, for he will save his people from their sins." (Matthew 1:19–21 ESV)

When Joseph woke up, he did as the angel of the Lord commanded him: he took his wife but held himself back from sexual relations until she had given birth to a son. And he called His name Jesus.

---

1. Luke 1:28–38 ESV

Elizabeth and her husband, Zechariah, were also visited by angels who foretold the purpose of their son's birth. They both surely erased their plans to spend their golden years in peace. They were about to have an active little-boy-turned-world-changing-man on their hands.

Today their lives are written in the Bible's red letters. John the Baptist, courageous and wild at heart, was the predecessor of Christ and became the first Christian martyr, beheaded by Herod, the king who was also an accessory to the murder of Jesus. And Jesus was the beloved Son of God, purposed before the foundation of the world as the Lamb to be slain for mankinds' sin.[2]

As His mother watched in agony, Jesus was beaten, whipped, nailed to a cross, and humiliated. Both Elizabeth and Mary became mothers at a surprising time, and their sons would achieve God's purposes on earth despite the pain it would cause them. They had found favor with God, but that did not excuse them from suffering. Being chosen would come at a price. Their hearts would be torn apart as the bodies of their sons were torn asunder. They would endure the singular pain of mothers who sacrifice their comfort for the sake of the kingdom. Their wombs were both troubling precipices and holy sanctuaries, the places through which God would carry His unfailing love into the world.

Our ministry's prayer coordinator has a daughter named Bethany. God also chose her to share a message through her womb. And He wrote a red-letter story she never would have penned herself. A new mother to their second son at the time of this writing, Bethany bore the pain of losing her first-born son, who changed the world and changed her. His name is Judah.

2. John 17:24; Revelation 13:8

Bethany's Story

Bethany and Adam had been married two and a half months when she discovered she had missed her period. The two, who married as virgins, had decided against using protection or pregnancy prevention methods out of obedience to a conviction from the Lord. They believed God had specifically asked them to trust Him with her womb and let Him fully write and plan their family's story.

Butterflies darted and flew in Bethany's heart as she and Adam awaited the results of the pregnancy test.

Was she ready to be a mommy?

She was twenty-one years old. Was that too young?

Would people judge them?

Was she ready for how this baby would change their lives forever?

How much she would love him? Adore him?

Who would this baby be?

These questions fluttered frantically as she and Adam held hands and looked to where the test lay nonchalantly on the windowsill beneath the blinds that swayed in the breeze. The little blue-and-white test shone in a shaft of sunlight.

Deep breath, eyes dizzy.

"Yes."

The room spun. Exclamation points exploded in her mind.

"Four to five weeks."

She and Adam laughed and cried at the same time. He held her, then knelt to her not-yet-swollen belly, leaning his forehead against it and praying over this little child quietly growing inside of her. They were three.

Soon the nausea began. If she wasn't vomiting, she was trying not to or wishing she could. Curled up in the fetal position, she questioned, "Should we have used birth control? Maybe we were wrong. Are we ready for this?" A human being was growing inside of her, and there was only one exit. The thought of labor struck fear in young Bethany.

But nothing could drown out the sweet dreams she had for their baby. She imagined who he or she would look like, Mommy or Daddy. She dreamed of the adventures they would have, the memories they'd make. How would this child change the world? Change *their* world? She felt aching twinges to meet their child and longed for the awe-filled moment of wonder when they would look upon their baby's face, when he or she would be warmth in her arms and not just a silent mystery. Her loving mama's heart began to bud and flourish.

Then, in the blink of an eye, she was twenty weeks along, and it was time to learn the sex.

The nurse squirted cold ultrasound gel over her growing abdomen and began to roll the probe. In a hushed, sacred moment, the baby boy turned over as if to look right into their souls and say, "Hello! I love you. I am yours." They looked right into his eyes and gazed at his little arms, legs, and tiny belly. He wiggled. This baby was perfect. Precious. Beautiful. They loved him with an unquenchable love.

Bethany almost didn't notice how silent the ultrasound tech became or how many measurements and pictures she took. Almost. The next morning she received a phone call that shattered their universe.

They needed to come see the doctor right away. "What's wrong?" Bethany asked, but the nurse could only fumble her words. "You and your husband just need to come today at noon."

"Should I call my husband at work and tell him he needs to be there with me?" Bethany asked.

"Yes."

All that was sure beneath Bethany's feet began to crumble. When Adam heard the sound of her indistinguishable sobs over the phone, he ran from the job site and jumped into his truck.

While she waited, a phone call came from the office of Maternal Fetal Medicine. *What in the world is that?* Bethany thought, frantic. The woman rattled off an address and wanted to know when to schedule her appointment. . .but Bethany told her she didn't know. Frantically she googled "maternal fetal medicine:" "High risk pregnancies. Babies with abnormalities, defects, or illness."

Something was wrong with her baby. Her perfect baby.

The Body-Soul Connection

There is a myth in our culture that our bodies are not connected to our souls, that bodies can be created and destroyed at our own will, and that bodies can be used as a means to an end; sexually, we can move from body to body to body with little to no soul impact. God assigned the first Adam and Eve a command: to be fruitful and multiply and fill the earth.

It is quite simple.

God created man.

God created woman to complement the man.

Together they reflect the image of God.

They leave father and mother.

Marry.

Cleave to one another.

Bear children.

Yet what have pornography, sexting, "friends with benefits," sexual immorality, prostitution, rape, molestation, and all the rest of the sexual perversion in our world done?

Denied God's commands.

People have become convinced He didn't really say that. He didn't really say man plus woman equals child, that we are made in His image and are to reproduce and fill the earth. No, people claim, what God really said is, "Anything goes. Do what feels good to you in the moment."

Right? Wrong. No, He didn't say that. He said: "For this reason a man shall leave his father and his mother, and be joined to his wife; and they shall become one flesh" (Genesis 2:24 NASB) and. . . "Be fruitful and multiply, and fill the earth, and subdue it" (Genesis 1:28 NASB).

Sexual perversion has been a part of our world ever since the first Adam left the garden. It is nothing new. The Internet has elevated sexual sin on the screens in front of our faces and on our tablets and the phones in our back pockets; and TV and movies have normalized it and made it look attractive and acceptable.

You just try telling young and faithful Bethany that her connection with Adam is not soul-to-soul, breath-to-breath, life-to-life, sanctified by God and holy to Him. You try telling Bethany her God is not the God of her womb, and that the love they have for Judah is not holy. Try telling her that her soul-to-soul connection with him has not birthed new life within her, and that life is not sacred. You just try telling her.

No movie, no pornographic film, no sex-trafficking ring, no Internet site that helps people cheat on their spouses, no politically correct law or statement by a politician or a movie star is going to change the beautiful, bottom-line truth: man and woman together reflect and create life.

What happens in our bodies happens in our souls.

Bethany's Pain

To set apart one's body for holiness is a beautiful gift back to the Savior who died for us. Yet this does not promise perfection in human terms; what is beautiful to God may seem deformed or decrepit to man.

"Our naive, innocent pregnancy bliss was a bombed-out shell," Bethany continues.

With bloodshot eyes, Adam and Bethany played checkers at a coffee shop to pass the time until they could see the doctor.

"I hated every step I took into the doctor's office. The sound of my feet hitting the floor pounded in my ears like a nightmare."

The doctor looked them in the eyes. "Your baby is not normal. The limbs are not the right length," she said. This baby's body was like one she'd never seen before. She would send them to a specialist in the Maternal Fetal Medicine office.

"I'm so sorry," she said and prayed with them.

The wind blew out of their souls. Everything seemed gray. Lifeless.

Adam wept as he told his mother. Bethany stared at the wall, eyes bleary. They called her parents. The grandparents' sobs over the speakerphone echoed off the walls of their living room in their little rental house. The sound of more dreams shattered. Everything they thought was sure was no more.

They had to be brave now.

The next morning Bethany tried to pull her socks and shoes on, to put on a brave face, to go to work, but she fell apart. *My little baby. . .is not okay. I was supposed to be a safe place for him. My body was meant to be his growing place. What happened? Was it something I did wrong?*

Within forty-eight hours they stepped into their new

doctor's office. Surely someone would have some answers.

With more ultrasound gel on her stomach, they looked closer at their baby and saw what they had missed out of pure, blind adoration: very short arms, very short legs. No fingers or toes.

"Do you want to know the gender?"

They nodded.

"It's a boy."

Bethany and Adam squeezed hands. This news would have been so thrilling before. The tech took lots of pictures and told them the doctor would be right in. But the doctor said he didn't know what was wrong with him. Their son did have severe anatomical abnormalities: a small chest, large belly, limbs that were measuring at nearly half what they should be, a missing nasal bone. . .but they would have to wait to know more. They did have options, the doctor said in his heavily accented, hard-to-understand tone.

"Termination."

Bethany's heart filled with terror. She felt helpless and alone, and those feelings became as much a part of that tiny room as the carpet and wallpaper. Whispers of defeat, failure, and fear told her there was no way out. The lies were so gripping, so choking, and so overpowering that she wondered if it is because of those suffocating, evil whispers that so many women say yes to termination.

Wendy's Story

Wendy was in college when she met a guy at the restaurant where she worked. She invited him over to her apartment, and the next thing she knew they were having sex. A few weeks later, she was tired, bloated, and out of sorts when she went to the campus nurse and described her symptoms. The nurse asked if Wendy might be pregnant and had her take a test. It came back positive. She started to panic. Fear filled her heart. The father was absolutely the worker at the restaurant. She did not know him, and he did not know her.

The nurse asked her when it happened—two weeks prior.

"Then it's early. You can get an abortion or have the baby," the nurse said. "You have some time to decide. But if you do plan to get an abortion, you will need to get one before three months, because after three months, it starts to become a baby." Before three months, she said, it was just a blob of tissue, and Wendy believed the whispering lie.

She called the guy from the restaurant. "I am pregnant, and you are the father."

All he said was, "So you are going to get an abortion, right?"

He didn't give her any other answer to fix the problem, so she said yes. Not even knowing that an abortion destroys a developing baby, she called the campus nurse back and told her she had made her decision.

At a secluded place off campus, Wendy was wearing a gown and lying on the table with her legs up. The nurse told her to focus on the mobile twirling above her head, not unlike the kind we put in nurseries to entertain our babies. The doctor told her she would hear a loud vacuuming sound and that he was going to vacuum out the tissue and she would feel some cramping. But she felt *a lot* of cramping and told the nurse it hurt *a lot*. But the nurse kept telling her, "You're doing great; just breathe through the pain. Focus on the mobile."

There was a lot of blood. They gave her a pad for the bleeding, and she got dressed. Her roommate brought her home.

In the car, her roommate asked, "So how do you feel?"

Waves of sadness washed over Wendy. She felt like someone inside her died. Instead of feeling relieved, she felt awful. She started to cry in the car.

"You should be happy you aren't pregnant anymore," her roommate said. "You'll be fine. Let's go get an ice cream."

They got out of the car, and there was a mom with a baby in a stroller.

Wendy looked at the baby and started crying uncontrollably; she could not catch her breath. For the rest of the day, she couldn't speak to anyone.

"I had so much pain in my heart I did not know how to express it or release it," she said.

The guy at the restaurant wanted to go out with her again, but she felt disgusting and sad. "I couldn't even think of going out with him," she said. "I was angry at him, at myself, at my roommate, and my life." She turned to food and alcohol for comfort. She stopped interacting with people. She couldn't think straight and felt spacey all the time. She fell into depression and started having suicidal thoughts.

Two years later, like so many women, she terminated another pregnancy, this time at a hospital so she could be put under and not see or hear anything.

"I really wanted to die at one point. This was when I felt the most alone."

But. . .

"God put a friend in my life who knew Him, and she invited me to church. At the end of the service, the pastor invited people who didn't know the Lord to come down to the altar and also invited those who had walked away from Him to come down and receive forgiveness for their sins. He shared Psalm 103:3 through 5 that says the Lord 'forgives all your iniquities and heals all your diseases, who redeems your life from the pit and crowns you with love and compassion, who satisfies your desires with good things. . . .'

"I went down to the front, kneeled at the altar, and overcome with sorrow, cried and asked God to forgive me for the abortions and help me change my life. I was so sorry for what I had done and became totally overwhelmed with God's love for me. At that time I gave my life fully to Him, and He filled me with a hunger to know Him more."

Bethany Wages War

"No. Termination is not a choice for us," Bethany and Adam said to the doctor, waging war against those whispers and fighting for their minds. For their son. For hope.

Later the doctor offered again, saying he needed to know soon, before termination became illegal at twenty-four weeks. But Bethany's dizzy mind just couldn't understand it. They didn't know what their son had. He had no medical diagnosis. They only knew he was disabled, that he wasn't "normal." He wasn't any danger to her. So she asked why this "option" was being pushed on them.

"Is his life not worth fighting for just because his body is deformed? Surely those with disabilities and defects—those who aren't 'normal'—are valuable human beings who have something beautiful to bring to this world!" Bethany cried.

They switched doctors. Bethany and Adam wanted someone to help them fight for the life of their son, to do everything possible to keep him healthy and safe; someone who would see the value in him, the love they had for him; someone who didn't want to cut his story short.

MYTH 8:

Abortion Is the Removal of Unwanted Tissue.

(Or so we've been told. . .)

—

TRUTH 8:

Abortion May Cause Trauma to the Soul.

(So here are the facts.)

LIFE VERSE:

The Word gave life to everything that was created.

JOHN 1:4 NLT

Beware

Beware of the wolf dressed in sheep's clothing. The situation looks good, sounds good, and feels good, but it is not good.

In Wendy's case, the guy at the restaurant where she worked after college flashed his eyes at her, drawing her in with his charming smile. The images flipped and turned like a slide show on fast forward, and two scenes later, she was having sex with him in her apartment. It's like sex scenes running across our eyes in films, but the pictures lie. Pictures make things look good that in real life aren't good at all. The apple we bite into bites us back.

Remember that Eve was deceived by a serpent with a slick-sounding voice. The lie of the enemy always makes it sound logical to disobey God. He convinces us to reject His warnings and makes them appear too confining—too controlling—too restrictive. Instead of embracing God's design as protective and loving and healthy and good, we believe the devil when he tells us God didn't really mean what He said. We trust the serpent when he tells us we would be better off being our own god, forging our own path.

The serpent didn't convince Eve by being wicked and mean; he persuaded her by appealing to her senses. He awakened Eve's eyes to the beauty of the tree, how pleasing it was to look at. Her mouth watered with desire. She hungered for power, to be wise in her own eyes. To be her own god.

But the tree that God told them not to eat from would open the hearts of the first couple to evil, inviting their own death. The Lord God didn't want that; He wanted to spend forever in His beautiful creation with the ones He loved. He wanted them to be free to choose. But in His heart He wanted them to walk along the rivers flowing through the valley of His creation. He wanted to celebrate life with Adam and Eve, the crown and glory of His hands and heart.

But curiosity got the best of them. They denied His Word and bit the apple. With the juice still dripping down their chins, hiding, fear, and shame became theirs.

God is only good. He cannot be in the presence of evil or sin. There is no shame in His holy place; no need to hide; no pain and no blame. There are no accusations or condemnation or disapproval or disease.

Forgiven and Set Free

Even after Wendy gave her life to the Lord and asked forgiveness from Him, she still carried the heavy weight of shame and wore the cloak of joylessness. Years later a friend stood up in church and boldly shared her abortion story, and Wendy knew she needed to get free. She began a Bible study with other post-abortive women called Forgiven and Set Free,[1] that helped her love her babies again, name them, mourn their losses, grieve, and forgive herself as well as everyone involved.

Miraculously, the loss of her children was not the end of her story. God enabled Wendy to fully receive His forgiveness and move on to a life of joy. Today she helps other women tell their stories and choose life in the fullness of Christ. At this moment, she is likely holding a young woman's hand, helping her to heal.

"God healed my heart and set me free from the guilt and shame. I realized He did not hold my abortions against me. I became free to have healthy relationships, free to live a life of joy in Jesus. Now I can say I am forgiven and set free to help others. . ."

1. Linda Cochrane, *Forgiven and Set Free* (Grand Rapids: Baker, 1996).

Abortion Facts[2]

♥ 1.2 million abortions are performed per year in the United States (that's 3,200 per day).

♥ More than fifty million legal, supervised abortions have occurred since abortion was legalized in 1973.

♥ Twenty-one percent of pregnancies end in abortions.

♥ One in five women have had abortions.

♥ Twenty-five percent of abortions occur around twelve weeks, when the baby has ten fingers, ten toes, a nose, eyes, and a mouth, and when all the organs—including a beating heart—are present.

♥ Only 12 percent of women report physical problems with their health among the reasons to have an abortion.

♥ One percent of aborting women report they were victims of rape.

The Warning Label

After talking to many women, reading their stories, and listening to them honestly share about the aftereffects of their abortions on ReviveOurHearts.com, I am convinced the Surgeon General needs a warning posted in all healthcare facilities about abortions, just like the ones you see about drinking alcohol while pregnant.

My "label" would simply state what science and the medical community have documented as true. It would be

2. National Abortion Federation Facts and Guttmacher Institute, "Abortion in the United States," guttmacher.org.

posted in doctor's offices, Planned Parenthood abortion clinics, government-funded healthcare centers, and hospitals.

Warning Label:

Abortions may cause guilt, anxiety, emotional numbness, depression, suicidal thoughts, eating disorders, or drug and alcohol abuse. Post-abortive women may also experience flashbacks of the procedure, fear of infertility, fear that future children will die, or difficulty being around children or pregnant women. Counseling can help the post-abortive person work through such essential nutrients for emotional health as forgiveness and love.

Research shows that women experience a trauma when they undergo an abortion, and the after-effects can be very similar to post-traumatic stress disorder, or PTSD—which is a serious condition that can develop after a person has experienced or witnessed a traumatic or terrifying event in which serious physical harm occurred. For most people, trauma can cause shock, anger, nervousness, fear, or guilt; and for most, these feelings go away after time. But for a person with PTSD, these feelings increase, becoming so strong that they keep the person from living a full life. People with PTSD cannot function as well as they did before the event occurred.[3]

The symptoms of post-abortion syndrome, also referred to as abortion PTSD, *do not happen to every person*, just as some people who have encountered war do not suffer

3. "Posttraumatic Stress Disorder," WebMD, last modified 2014, http://www.webmd.com/mental-health/post-traumatic-stress-disorder.

from PTSD. If they do occur, these symptoms will not necessarily appear at the same time, and neither are women likely to experience the entire list. Some symptoms may occur immediately after an abortion, and others can show up years later.[4]

Symptoms of Abortion Post-Traumatic Stress Disorder

- ♡ Guilt. A mother's heart is genetically designed to "protect her child at all costs." Abortion short-circuits that basic human instinct. This can lead to feelings of guilt.

- ♡ Anxiety. Many women start feeling tense and cannot relax. Dizziness, pounding heart, upset stomach, and headaches may occur. They may worry about the future, struggle to concentrate, and not be able to sleep.

- ♡ Avoiding children or pregnant women. Some women avoid pregnant mothers or children. This avoidance can include skipping baby showers, walking around the block to avoid a playground, or making excuses to escape events that include pregnant women or children.

- ♡ Feeling "numb." To avoid painful thoughts, many women shut off their emotions. This could mean abandoning friendships and family, particularly if they remind them of their past.

- ♡ Depression. Everyone is sad once in a while. After abortion, gloomy feelings can make a woman feel hopeless and unlovable. She may cry uncontrollably for no reason and/or feel like she is going crazy. Perhaps she can't eat or sleep. Others eat too much

4. Taken from Dr. Paul and Teri Reisser in their book *Help for the Post-Abortive Woman* (now entitled *A Solitary Sorrow*), posted here: "Abortion PTSD Symptoms," Ramah International, http://ramahinternational.org/abortion-ptsd-symptoms/.

and sleep all day. They avoid the things they used to enjoy.

♥ Thoughts of suicide. Some post-abortive women get so sad they think it would be easier to die. Others miss their lost child so much that they want to join them to hold them at last.

♥ Anniversary reminders. This "anniversary" can be the aborted child's due date or the date of the abortion. On these dates, individuals can feel horrible for no apparent reason.

♥ Flashbacks. A post-abortive woman can be suddenly transported back to the procedure and remember everything in her mind. Memories can be triggered by simple sounds like a vacuum cleaner, a dentist drill, or a toilet flushing. Others experience ongoing nightmares.

♥ Fear of infertility. A common reaction after abortion is to worry about being able to get pregnant again. Many fear they have aborted the only child they will ever have.

♥ Unable to bond with their children. If women have kids before or after the abortion, these can be a constant reminder of the person they aborted. This pain can result in the woman distancing herself at an emotional level or believing she is disqualified to be a parent.

♥ Fear that future children will die. Some post-abortive people live in fear that children they had before or after the abortion could easily die. This fright can lead these parents to overprotect their children at an unhealthy level.

♥ Eating disorders. Episodes of anorexia or bulimia are common. Some overeat or undereat to avoid anyone wanting them at a sexual level as that could lead to another pregnancy. Controlling food is a grasp for control when life feels overwhelming.

♥ Alcohol and drug use. Drugs and alcohol often serve

as a tranquilizer to help keep the memories at a distance. They can help calm anxiety and promote sleep. Sadly, the overuse of these elements can lead to other problems on a mental and physical level.

Go Tell It

In the amazing book *Go Tell It,* many post-abortive women share their stories. The chance to work at pregnancy resource centers leads many women to transform their pain into purpose. The truth is that post-abortive women help the most women choose life. These women are helping others find their voice and their value. The answer is not one single Bible study or one class. The answer is surrounding oneself with compassionate, caring women. Together we help each other heal.[5]

God tells us our bodies are not meant for sexual immorality, but for the Lord. He is saying, "I want to live in the temple of you. I want to fill your body with life." No pain is too great that He cannot heal it. He *can* heal. He *will* redeem. There *is* hope.

> The LORD is merciful and gracious. . . . He does not deal with us according to our sins, nor repay us according to our iniquities. For as high as the heavens are above the earth, so great is his steadfast love toward those who fear him; as far as the east

---

5. I highly recommend listening to the story of Nancy Lincoln on ReviveOurHearts.com, who provided much information for this writing, as well as visiting OptionOnline.org or ramahinternational.org for post-abortion grief assistance in your area. Bible study recommendations are: *Forgiven and Set Free* by Linda Cochrane; *Healing the Father's Heart* by Linda Cochrane; *Her Choice to Heal* by Sydna Masse; and *Surrendering the Secret* by Pat Laden. Suggested retreats are: Rachel's Vineyard (Catholic) and Deeper Still (nondenominational).

is from the west, so far does he remove our transgressions from us. As a father shows compassion to his children, so the LORD shows compassion to those who fear him. For he knows our frame; he remembers that we are dust. (Psalm 103:8–14 ESV)

MYTH 9:

The Body and Soul Are Separate.

(One doesn't affect the other.)

—

TRUTH 9:

The Body and Soul Are Connected.

(An experience in one is an experience in the other.)

LIFE VERSE:

*And let me live whole and holy,
soul and body, so I can always walk
with my head held high.*

Psalm 119:30 msg

Written in the Sand

No one really knows what Jesus wrote in the sand the day He bent down in the center of town with the mob fuming and the broken lady in the middle. For some reason I think He was writing her destiny in the sand—her real name and true identity—because no matter how much life shakes its finger at us, blaming and shaming us for our not-enoughness, accusing us of our sin, He calls us by name. He doesn't call us Adulteress, Cheat, Liar, Deformed, or the One Who Had an Abortion. He calls us Loved, Chosen, Forgiven, Redeemed, Destined for More.

Soul-Oneness

As much as we can't always grasp it, there is always purpose in the pain we bear—and what happens in the body happens in the soul. The woman caught in adultery affected not only her marriage but her soul and her husband's soul. It wasn't just about sex. It was a violation of the sanctity of marriage, of soul-oneness, of what happens when two become one.

And when two become one, one plus one equals two. People are joined and babies are formed and their souls are never the same.

I've been surprised by this book, by how much it has to do with babies.

What does sex have to do with babies? They are inextricably combined—colors on the same canvas. One bleeds into another; they just cannot be separated, though we may try.

Sex is an expression of affection, commitment, whole-knowing, intimacy, respect, adoration, and love between two people—and marriage is ideally consummated after the wedding day, after the couple has pronounced their commitment to one another in front of family and friends and celebrated.

This is the picture of married love we are shooting for, and the goal we have in mind—for young brides and grooms to become more the norm than the exception—for purity to return to the bedroom. "Marriage should be honored by all, and the marriage bed kept pure" (Hebrews 13:4 NIV).

Our goal, too, is to remember that sex makes babies—this was God's first command to the first couple—to cling to another, to leave father and mother and be one, and to fill the earth with their children and children's children. It is the ultimate picture of God's design for marriage.

Sex and children are intertwining threads of the same tapestry. Melding brushstrokes of distinct color on the same canvas: sex, the sky; the children, stars.

Judah's Destiny

So what happened to Bethany's baby, and does his light still shine?

She had to face the hard truth: she had a child with disabilities. She wondered: Would their son take his first steps or speak his first words? Would his little limbs fit into the cute onesies she had lovingly selected for his registry? What would the rest of their lives look like, taking care of him? Carrying him to the bathroom, helping him shower? Would they see him come home from school, face tearstained and eyes full of failure and worthlessness due to bullying? Could they afford the wheelchairs, the doctor and physical therapy appointments?

Would they even get to bring him home from the hospital?

There lay her greatest fears and worst nightmares. Those who had saved sex for marriage could not write their own destinies or predict their own futures. They could only bow, cry, trust, and plead with God to complete His work within them. Sometimes God changes His mind on account of our pleas; sometimes His purpose stands.[1] Breathless sobs played on repeat for the next two months. It was in one of those times of rawness before God that Adam asked the Lord, "Who is this child? What is his name?"

"Judah Rees."

"Okay, but, Rees isn't even a family name. . .why Rees?"

They looked up the names. Together the names meant "passionate praise of the Lord" or "running to praise."

In a moment prior to walking into the initial ultrasound, before they even knew a hint of Judah's deformity, the Holy Spirit spoke a verse to Adam about their child—a seemingly random verse that didn't make sense at the time but now brought a word of hope.

"Behold, I and the children whom the Lord hath given me are for signs and for wonders in Israel from the Lord of hosts" (Isaiah 8:18 KJV).

Wonders. Signs. What happens in the body happens in the soul. So their souls would keep crying out for miracles. They purposed in their hearts to stop mourning a son whom they had not yet lost.

At their twenty-eight-week appointment, baby Judah turned over, wiggled, and kicked his arms and legs. He practiced breathing and hiccuped like Bethany had felt him do inside her so many times. Judah's fighting spirit brought a smile to Bethany's face and a hopeful breeze to her heart.

But the doctor told them that Judah had a lethal

---

1. See Isaiah 14:24.

condition, meaning he would die. Bethany squinted her eyes tight and willed herself to breathe as part of her died. The bombshell threw her against the wall, and darkness settled over her soul.

From Darkness to Light

Judah's chest was too small and his heart too big for his lungs to breathe once he was born. That is, if he made it to birth at all. There was a 99 percent chance he would die before then, but the doctor vowed to follow Bethany and Adam every step of the way and fight for that 1 percent.

Bethany quietly canceled her baby shower and asked for the miracle of healing a thousand more times. Then she and Adam turned to desperate praise in the deepest, darkest places of their souls. No amount of Netflix, comfort food, distractions, or coffee could ease the ache. His microscopic hiccups would bring an involuntary smile to his mama's face, then immediate tears as she would lay her head down on her hands and try to memorize how his movements felt.

Then one day—*pop*, her water broke. At thirty weeks. With a disabled son who already had very minimal chances of survival, he would now be a preemie.

"God, *why*?" Bethany cried, the moaning sob bleeding from her lips, full of agony, as liquid drained around her in pools. The amniotic fluid that was Judah's playground flooded to the floor.

Blankly they ran through the snow to the car, her pants soaked in the freezing cold. They brought Judah's onesie and blanket, in hopes that just maybe they could bring him home.

In the waiting room, she fumbled to put on a hospital

gown. Sweet girl had no idea what was going to happen; she had no birth plan. But the nurses stopped the labor, explaining that the longer Judah's lungs and brain could develop, the better. With every twelve-hour shift change, Bethany and Adam had to answer questions from new nurses and hear new advice, often the opposite of what they had heard before. Every night, they passed out completely drained, Adam clutching Judah's blanket, dried tears coating their faces, heavyhearted from the impossible decisions that faced them as surely as the heart monitors beeped.

The doctors said the two of them could go home and let nature take its course, so they made a "jailbreak" and returned to the comfort of home to wait and see what would happen. They sat on their sunny kitchen floor and had a picnic with their favorite snacks while they let worship songs wash over them and Judah. The second night home, the contractions began again, and she went into full labor. It was over. They could not hold off any longer. In sickness or in health, alive or dead, they were going to meet their son.

"Labor hit me full on, and nothing could have prepared me for the pain of it. The strength of it. Both epidural attempts failed. I could now, perhaps mercifully, think of nothing else besides surviving each contraction and the sound of my own breathing as Adam held my hands. The encouraging coaching of my cousin and looking into Adam's sure, safe eyes was what gave me courage to bear the unbearable, to get me to the next moment. I began to push.

"'You're about to meet your son!' my cousin said with courage.

"One last push, and there he was. They quickly handed him to NICU doctors, then shortly afterward he was placed in my arms, skin to skin, just like I had requested. 'Is there anything you can do to help him? Does he need a ventilator?' I asked. The NICU doctors looked at each other and shook their heads. I knew what that meant. He was not going to make it.

"But as I held his tiny body, we realized what a miracle he was. He was *alive*. He looked like he had really been through it, but he had fought. His limbs were indeed deformed, joints not like others', but he had beautiful fingers and toes and a perfect, handsome nose. He had made it. We watched his heart beat right in front of us. His eyes were wide open. He had fought through the difficulty and exhaustion of labor just so we could greet him, look in his eyes, and touch his beating heart while we whispered, 'I love you' over and over into his ears that looked just like his daddy's. We wrapped him in the blanket his great-grandma had made for him. I touched his head full of dark hair and his face over and over, memorizing it with my fingers. A great peace and calm washed over me."

Adam gave Judah a bath and put on a tiny preemie diaper that was still too big for him, and they watched as his heartbeat slowly declined. After about thirty minutes of drinking him in and holding him in their warm embrace, they said good-bye.

Judah Lives

The memorial service was packed. Everyone sang many of the worship songs they had sung with Judah in the womb. People who had perhaps seldom thought about the purpose and value of life were suddenly confronted by a little child whose lungs had never filled with oxygen, who had lived just thirty minutes, yet who had changed so many and had a funeral more full of people than some who live to old age.

A tiny, deformed child's life begged the questions of all present: Why am I here? What makes me valuable? What matters while I'm here on earth? What am I doing with what little time I am here?

People saw two broken, very ordinary and very young parents standing by their son's tiny casket and praising God through their tears. Many people left that room changed that day, many whose souls had been brushed against and beckoned by the powerful and mysterious whisper of the Holy Spirit, invited to live a life so much deeper and more remarkable, to be free of the hopelessness, the mundane, and the monotonous.

Bethany closes: "What might seem incredulous is that his life was worth everything. Every stab of grief. Every attack of nausea and vomiting. Every sleepless, tear-filled night, every foggy, sob-filled day. Every dream destroyed. Every excruciating contraction. Even holding him for the last time, saying good-bye, the most searing pain, the darkest hell, and every day of the rest of our earthly lives we will spend with a gaping hole in our hearts. . . . I would do it all a million times over for his beautiful, wonderful, deformed body, his face that looked more like his daddy's. For that big heart pounding in that tiny chest. The little boy who is still making our lives so sweet, so meaningful, who makes us so proud to be his parents and made heaven feel so much more near.

"Judah taught us to praise more passionately than before, to take more risks, to find our value as humanity not in our jobs, our age, our education, our exterior, or our 'achievements.' He taught us to love adamantly, unapologetically, and fiercely, like Jesus loves us. His frame and life were, by the world's estimation, so small and so fragile, but his testimony is so very big and strong and still continues to reach out.

"We love you, Judah Rees St. Marie. We miss you deeply and dream of the day when we will hold you again and run with you to praise our God. You were so beautiful and perfect, exactly as you were, exactly as you are. Thank you for fighting for us, little son. You were, without a doubt, so worth it."

MYTH 10:

Being Sexually Active Won't Hurt Me.

(Or anybody else.)

~

TRUTH 10:

Anything Outside of God's
Best for You Hurts.

(Watch out for the wolves dressed like sheep.)

LIFE VERSE:

"You will recognize them by their fruits."

MATTHEW 7:20 ESV

Beware of the Wolves

Why is it that we cherish a long-standing line of children's stories that include wolves gobbling up little people? Honestly, it's so strange that we put children to bed reading stories about the Big Bad Wolf. But our little boy loves these stories—out of an entire album of children's books, he loves to read the ones with the wolves! Whether the wolf is terrorizing little pigs, devouring baby sheep, or eating Little Red Riding Hood alive, we gotta wonder what's up with these wolves in disguise.

Jesus said, "Beware of false prophets, who come to you in sheep's clothing but inwardly are ravenous wolves" (Matthew 7:15 ESV). The situation *looks* good but is *not good.* When Jesus says "beware," I think He's trying to get our attention—for He is good, He calls Himself the Good Shepherd—and He can see right through dangerous situations for His sheep. He tells us: "The thief comes only to steal and kill and destroy. I came that they may have life and have it abundantly. I am the good shepherd. The good shepherd lays down his life for the sheep" (John 10:10–11 ESV).

I am so glad He doesn't call us pigs. He calls us sheep! Sheep are cute, but they only survive when they stick with the flock, when they have a caring shepherd who watches over them. Jesus says if *anyone* but a good shepherd is in charge of the sheep, such as a hired man, that man will run when he sees the wolf coming, because he doesn't love the sheep. Guess what happens when a good shepherd isn't there? The wolf will snatch them and scatter them![1]

A good shepherd will also go far and away to recover one lost sheep, because she is valuable to him and being

1. John 10:12

separated from the flock makes her vulnerable to the wolves. When he finds that one sheep, he will carry her back on his shoulders into the safety of the pasture.

"Beware of the wolves. . . ."

The sign says, BEWARE. You have to be shrewd and ask the Holy Spirit for wisdom to see through people and situations, because wolves often come dressed in sheep's clothing, making themselves look good, but if you trust them they could eat you alive.

Little Red Riding Hood

In the story of Little Red Riding Hood, the little girl is sent off by her mother to bring a basket of cookies to her grandmother, and she meets the wolf along the way. She is alone, separated from family and community, when she is sent off with a goal in mind—a good goal. But when she meets the wolf, he talks in syrupy, sweet words, convincing her he is good and has the best of intentions for her.

She sinks her teeth into the wolf's lies and allows him to redirect her path (even though her mother told her to make no stops along the way). So now she finds herself doing something the wolf told her to do—picking flowers for her grandmother—which sounds good, looks good, feels good.

But the wolf is way ahead of her. He sneaks ahead to try to demolish her future. He tricks the grandmother and swallows her alive. Then he tricks Little Red Riding Hood into believing he is the grandmother (how a wolf poses as a grandma in a bonnet, we'll never know!). Foolish Red Riding Hood doesn't recognize the wolf in disguise, and he eats her, too. What a comforting bedtime tale for a child!

The incredible ending is that a passing hunter sees the wolf for who he is, whips out his knife, and with an exacting blade, cuts open the wolf's gut, and out hop the little girl and her grandma, unscathed. At the end of the story, they are enjoying a nice cup of tea and those delicious cookies!

So here we have a young lady sent away from home; a wolf who pretends again and again to be a good guy; and a hunter who saves the day.

Sounds a little like my story.

The Truth about Your Body

When I was a model, starting at the age of eight and then more seriously from ages fifteen to twenty-two, I believed many of the myths in this book. During high school and college, I believed that what I did with my body was up to me—and in a way, it was! God does give us the freedom to choose. But it never occurred to me that my body was not my possession—that God made it and wanted to be Lord of it—that it could be His home. I did not realize that how I behaved in my body affected my Maker, my heavenly Father, my parents, and the people I would love in the future. In the modeling world, people critiqued my body as if it were a painting they could evaluate.

Believing my body and soul to be separate, I was like a woman in a foggy daze. I harmed my body and therefore my soul. I may have been a straight-A student, but in life, I was on a roller coaster of insecurity.

I did not know what my true value was. I did not know God calls us "pearls of great value," and that our worth is found in Him. I did not know God calls our bodies "temples," and we are to protect our bodies like we would the house of God. That's the real reason to "flee from sexual immorality," by the way—to protect our hearts from shame, heartbreak, and pain—as well as disease and potential death, as you'll see in the chapters on sexually transmitted diseases.

By guarding our bodies, we are protecting our hearts—and everything we do in life is an overflow of the heart (Proverbs 4:23).

Because the body and soul are so connected, girls who give their bodies away end up extremely unhappy, and often don't know why. They don't realize how the choices they make in their bodies now will affect their souls later. Not only do many girls treat their bodies like their own possessions, but they also allow boys or men to treat it like their possessions. Outside the loving covenant of marriage, this only leads to heartache and harm (no matter what the movies say). . .leaving girls in pain and all alone, time and again.

This kind of thing doesn't happen all at once. It happens instance by instance, like chipping at a stone wall until it is a pile of rubble. There's the first chip, the next chip, the next. Not one single explosion—just a slow chipping until the final blow crumbles the heart.

As I hit my early twenties, I also tried to control my body so it would measure up to the perfection expected of models—which also affected my soul. I began not feeding my body well, over exercising, and taking diet pills to meet the standard of the world of fashion. I walked the runway in Europe, appeared in magazines, TV commercials, and advertising campaigns—which put extraordinary emphasis on my outward appearance and left little room for me to nurture my heart.

But our bodies don't ever reach perfection, and if the

moment of perfection comes, it flees away like a skittish bird. It is here, then gone.[2]

When we believe the myth that our bodies are our possessions, it starts out kind of like a party, but the whole thing ends up in tears. We live a selfish lie, and then we and everyone we love pays the price. Women and girls who have lived this lie will tell you it hurts, because our bodies are connected to our souls, and anything outside of God's best for us hurts. When we give our bodies away or harm them in any way, we hurt our souls and the souls who are tied to us. It's that simple.

So how does a powerful trance like this get broken in a broken girl? That's also simple.

Jesus moves in. Yes, He moves in to the dilapidated, messed-up, given-away body and says, "Let's clean house." If the house He moves into is in disarray, He is still quite happy to move in. When I accepted Christ, my soul was hurting. My mind was like a hornet's nest—confused, scattered, buzzing this way and that, stinging me and everyone near it. My heart was a shattered vase. My body was filled with darkness. When I looked in the mirror, the eyes staring back at me were hazy veils of shadows, a foggy, stormy night.

My Story

When I received Christ as my Lord and Savior, I immediately saw the connection between body and soul. I had lived my whole life believing my body was my possession, and

2. The whole crazy story of my search for perfection is in my first book, *Girl Perfect*. If you struggle with body image, the real definition of beauty, and where we find true fulfillment, the pages of that book were written just for you.

then in one moment, *snap*: I knew it wasn't. The lightbulb went on. *"Hello?"* said the Holy Spirit. *"I'm here now. I've moved in, and I'm going to treat this place like it's holy as gold, pure as glass."*

The sacredness of my body was established fact. I realized so much: my health mattered to God, my sexuality mattered to God, even my job mattered to God. So I quit modeling right away, because showing off my looks was in direct opposition to the truth of my soul. It was easy to walk away; I wanted God's best and nothing less. Over time my health was restored, my mind was restored, and my future became bright.

God does not come and invade your soul like a robber looking to steal. He knocks. When invited into a person's heart, He takes us as we are, with all the dirt in the corners, the aching and breaking and unholy. Over time He takes back the pain and turns it around like the sun wiping out the cloudy mess.

That was the girl who met the Cowboy, the girl who had her canvas washed white as the snow, soul paper clean. That was the girl who clutched a bouquet of blushed roses and floated down a pure white aisle scattered with petals, the girl draped in a gown of white satin, hand-embroidered train of pearls trailing behind, the girl whose daddy lifted the veil and presented her to her groom.

Have I mentioned the Cowboy is also a hunter?

I was now in the arms of a faithful man, a man of God, a man who waited to have sex with me until marriage, a man who would hunt for the hurt in me and partner with God to heal it.

How do you tell the difference between a wolf and a hunter? The wolf is interested in the exterior—what he can take from you. But the hunter looks beyond what he can see to the interior and carefully extracts life from that which appears dead and gone.

The wolf devours life; while the hunter values life. The wolf steals what is innocent and good, but the hunter searches for life, breaks it, and gives it back as a blessing.

MYTH 11:

Casual Sex Is Possible.
(One-night stands last for one night.)

—

TRUTH 11:

Sex Is Not Casual; Sex Is Binding.
(Flee!)

LIFE VERSE:

Flee from sexual immorality. Every other sin a person commits outside the body, but the sexually immoral person sins against his own body.

1 CORINTHIANS 6:18 ESV

Flee!

Pretend your apartment is on fire and you are in it. You touch the door and it burns your palms, which means the flames are in the hallway. You are on the fourteenth floor, so the window is not an option; you have one escape route, the back stairs. But you hear screams and cries down the stairwell. What do you do?

Touch up your makeup? Take a selfie? Casually walk to the stairwell?

No. You flee! You run like a woman with her pants on fire, taking the only escape route you have. Do you walk casually, stopping to make small talk? No. You *flee*!

When the Bible says to "flee" from something, God is telling you to run like a madwoman to a place of safety; He is telling you to take heed—this is life or death for your soul. The same word the Bible uses in the verse "*flee* from sexual immorality" (1 Corinthians 6:18) is the same word in "Resist the devil and he will *flee* from you" (James 4:7), and the same word for the hired hand that *flees* the sheep because the wolves are coming (John 10:12).

Sexual sins are unique because they...

♥ tap into the deepest aspects of our emotions

♥ compromise our most valuable human relationships (family, marriage, friendship)

♥ breach trust

♥ produce guilt

♥ give rise to other immoral behavior

♥ ultimately assault the lordship of Jesus Christ

The Soul-to-Soul Connection

If what happens in the body happens in the soul, how does sex outside of marriage affect the soul?

Wendy shares her experience. "I never saw a film in school or heard a teaching that every person whom I was intimate with would be in my marriage bed. And I didn't know I would develop a soul tie with every person I was intimate with."

My friend Nikki describes the terror of her husband's pornography usage and multiple affairs. She writes, "It was like I was in bed with so many other women."

If sex is soul to soul, then soul-to-soul connections can be made prior to marriage, and these connections have potential to cause damage to a future marriage. Sexual experiences create strong emotional memories that can live far beyond the moment—even into marriage.

Sexual sins are unique because they tap into our deepest emotions, affect our most valuable relationships, break trust, produce guilt, and lead to more immorality; they are different than other sins—they are carried in the body. . . they are a sin against the soul. You can't wash them off or drown them out, no matter how hard you try.

Many years after college, Wendy was deeply affected by her memories of sexual sin. She carried soul ties and curses that tormented her, causing tremendous grief and pain that prevented her from living a joyful life, even as a wife and mom. Before Christ enters into a painful part of our past, every time we recall that memory, we feel mental and emotional anguish—but when we are healed, pain is no longer associated with that memory. We don't forget; but when we do remember, we do not feel pain any longer.

In search of healing, Wendy learned about a ministry called Sozo, which is named after a Greek word occurring

110 times in the New Testament.[1]

Sozo means "whole"; more specifically, it means "saved, healed, and delivered"—and that was exactly what Wendy needed. Through this ministry, she broke the soul ties that were binding her.

What Are Soul Ties?

Your soul is your mental capacity to have thoughts, your ability to make choices, and the emotions you feel. It is your thinker, your chooser, and your feeler.

So what is a soul tie? A soul tie is a relational connection to another human being. Human beings are wired for connection and created for relationship. We have *healthy* soul ties with people that produce genuine love, joy, and peace. These relationships are God ordained. They can be between husband and wife, with family, church, or close friends.

We can have *unhealthy* soul ties, too. Unhealthy connections between people result in guilt, shame, and anger and even occupy our thoughts to the point that we cannot embrace life to the fullest. Relational connections are tested by their *fruit*. Good soul ties bear good fruit—and bad soul ties bear bad fruit. Check out the chart that follows to test the fruit of your connections.[2]

Your soul is:
- ♡ your intellect (your thinker)
- ♡ your will (your chooser)
- ♡ your emotions (your feeler)

You think; you choose; you feel. . .that is your soul.

1. http://bethelsozo.com
2. Material adapted from "Understanding Soul Ties" by Patrice Sampley, MA, LPC (Lifegale Solutions, Colleyville, TX, Spring 2003).

Good Soul Connections produce:

Love   Blessing   Loyalty   Honor   Fidelity
Righteousness   God's Order   Peace

The Result of Good Soul Ties is emotional wholeness.

Bad Soul Connections produce:

Manipulation   Anger   Strife   Control   Resentment
Emotional Enslavement   Hatred   Abuse (emotional, physical, mental, sexual)
Damaging or Illicit Sexual Behavior
Codependent Tendencies (thinking you can't function without the
other person's permission or approval)
Enablement (making excuses for another person's poor choices)
Rescuing Behavior (thinking you can rescue someone from their problems)
Curses (believing the enemy's lies about who you are and agreeing
with the devil about your destiny and purpose)

Bad Soul Ties hold us back from experiencing
the abundant life God wants for us.

Cleaning House

Remember how in the Garden of Eden there was no shame or blame? No guilt or manipulation, *until* the serpent convinced Eve to attach herself to his words instead of God's? This is what unhealthy soul connections do for us: they do the damaging work of separating us from God's truths. They bind us so much we cannot believe or obey His Word. They also separate us from our true soul mates. In Eve's case, that was her husband. In the case of single people, children, teenagers, widows, and orphans, the soul still needs good, healthy ties! Marriage is just one of those promise-driven relationships that connects our hearts, minds, and decisions to another person. Familial soul ties can also be very strong—some are great! Like when Ruth says to Naomi in the book of Ruth, "Where you go I will go. . . . Your people shall be my people" (1:16 ESV). That is a healthy relational tie, and hopefully we have good healthy friendships and relationships like this.

But there are some ties with family members, friends, churches, or boyfriends that hurt us deeply. Those ties can still linger in the back corners of our souls, whispering lies to us about who we are in Christ. Some relationships make us feel so badly about ourselves, so guilty, so not-enough, that they can set up whole shops inside of us and operate without us even knowing it.

Cleaning out your soul is kind of like cleaning the fridge. You open it up and look at what's inside. On the surface, it might look fine—maybe a little messy and disorganized—but when you start digging, oh, the stuff you find! The grit in the back corners, the too-old soup, the milk gone bad, the leftovers that stink when you pop open the lid. You start with one thing, then you find yourself emptying out the whole fridge (and freezer, too), wiping down the shelves and reorganizing it in a way that is pretty on the surface and fresh on the inside.

As Jesus said, "First clean the inside of the cup. . .that the outside also may be clean" (Matthew 23:25–26 ESV).

When you clean out the fridge, you take out the garbage. This is the happy moment when you throw away the old and moldy and keep the yummy and good. Then, when you walk back into the house and make lunch, you are satisfied because you have cleaned things from within.

To have a full life (and that includes your sex life if you marry), you want your soul to be rid of any unhealthy attachments.

Sex is a flesh-to-flesh, soul-to-soul, and heart-to-heart connection. It is not like the casually stated relationship of "friends with benefits." This shallow phrase was coined by those who think "casual sex" is possible. But there is nothing casual about sex!

In marriage, sex forges a magnetic bond between man and wife. Like two magnets coming together, sex ignites the desire to be with my husband more; it produces emotional attachment. It conveys affection and affirmation. It is a way of building each other up and making each other feel loved and valuable.

When this is done by force or through coercion, it is sinful. When motivated by lust or the desires of the flesh, without the covenant promise of faithfulness—it creates a soul tie that doesn't belong there. (This is why Jesus tells us to flee from them!)

Breaking Soul Ties

If you feel like you have some unhealthy attachments to people or experiences that are preventing you from experiencing the joy and peace that can be found in Christ, you have the authority to break those ties. That does not necessarily mean you break the relationship. You may keep the relationship but sever the tie of guilt and shame from it. If it is a God-ordained relationship that causes you to have unhealthy reactions like anger and fear, you can break the unhealthy attachment and keep the relationship; it all depends on whether it is good for you or not.

If the relationship, past or present, is not God ordained, blessed, and sanctified by the healthy fruit this relationship brings to your life, then the ungodly soul tie should be severed. A Christian counselor or Sozo center would be a great resource for you in this area.[3]

3. Information about counseling centers, breaking soul ties, and Sozo centers can be found on my website, urmore.org/facts.php.

Since you are a daughter of the King, with Christ living inside of you, you have the authority to demolish strongholds yourself. Strongholds are just that: strong holds. They are things that have a *strong hold* on you—and can occupy your mind, live in your heart, and influence your actions in a negative way.

Here's How You Break a Soul Tie:

♥ First, ask the Lord if you have any bad soul ties. He will reveal them to you by showing you the fruit of the relationship.

♥ Confess with your mouth—say out loud the connection that is hurting you, by naming the person or memory and identifying how this connection makes you feel. Say out loud what you experience as a result of this bond, "This bond makes me feel _____."

♥ Confess your responsibility for your own actions—have you done anything to contribute to this bond that is wrong? Name your own sin, and ask forgiveness for it.

♥ Forgive the other person for his or her part in the equation. "I forgive _____ for making me feel _____ and for _____."

♥ Pray sincerely that the soul tie be severed—"In the name of Jesus Christ, I break my bonding and connection with _____ and cut the ungodly soul tie I have with this person (or experience) that is stealing from my life."

♥ Pray for the stronghold to be removed—"I demolish the effect this tie has had on my mind, my will, and my emotions. I refuse to take on the negative characteristics, tendencies, or influences I have received from this bond; I take every thought captive into the obedience of Jesus Christ."

♥ Command the enemy to flee from you, and give your soul to Jesus.

♥ Ask the Holy Spirit to clean you from the inside out—"Purify my heart, Lord. Cleanse my mind. Align my will with Yours. Restore my heart."[4]

---

4. Material adapted from "Understanding Soul Ties" by Patrice Sampley, MA, LPC (Lifegale Solutions, Colleyville, TX, Spring 2003).

MYTH 12:

Sexually Transmitted Diseases Are Shameful.

(And only sinful people get them.)

~

TRUTH 12:

Sexually Transmitted Diseases Are Very Contagious.

(And lots of young people have them and don't realize it.)

LIFE VERSE:

It is my eager expectation and hope that I will not be at all ashamed, but that with full courage now as always Christ will be honored in my body, whether by life or by death.

PHILIPPIANS 1:20 ESV

What I Wish I Knew Before I Kissed a Boy

"This is what I wish I knew before I kissed a boy," Wendy says. "I wish I knew there is a potential of developing a disease that is incurable. I wish I knew that I could pass that disease on to another person whom I was intimate with." Wendy started to get cold sores on her lips over the years. Not understanding what was causing them, she went to the doctor. The doctor told her it was a herpes virus disease, or HSV-17 and it affects the lips and face. Wendy contracted it from someone and then passed it on to her husband. Herpes is a viral disease that is treatable but not curable, and Wendy and her husband have had to deal with the repercussions of her sexual activity in her college years, even now that she is a devoted wife, mom, prayer warrior, and mentor. Not only did Wendy have emotional scars, but like Boo, she had a physical reminder that scarred her.

Ditch the Stigma

I'm going to be honest with you. I originally started this chapter with facts and warnings and fear-inducing statements about STDs and why you don't ever want one. The truth is, STDs are harmful, and you need to be warned, and we are going to do that. But when I read Paige's story, I found myself crying in my office, that slobbery, messy cry that a girl barely recovers from. I wanted to fall down on the floor and tell God, "I really can't do this!"

But He says I can, so I will.

STDs are not shameful. They are sexually transmitted diseases, and they are real. And we've got to understand them!

But good education starts with this: we all have hearts beating in our chests. We all want to live life to the full. We all have dreams and aspirations, and we all get a raw deal at some point in life. Paige will tell you—as will Wendy and Boo—that STDs don't make you dirty or worthless. Sexually transmitted diseases are diseases, not statements of your value.

Are there ways to avoid them? If you were not born with them, then yes, there are ways to protect yourself.

But first, drop your rocks.

We are all children of God, all loved, and there is no shame or condemnation. God loves us so much He sent His Son to take the penalty for our perversion. He took the beating for us. Because of Him, we dare not beat others, isolate, or point fingers at people on account of their diseases. Let's not heap shame on shame, but grace on grace, like Jesus did.

No one's life ever changed in a good way because of accusation or judgment.

Lives are changed for the better by grace and truth.

The Word teaches us to seek wisdom. Seek understanding. Seek knowledge. For he who runs from knowledge is a fool, but he who seeks understanding is wise.

So if you or anyone you know has an STD, know this. . . we care. Our hearts are filled with compassion, concern, and caution. And we need *you* to be a voice for girls like us. Because we believe you, too, can change the world.

Seek Wisdom. Pursue Understanding. Acquire Knowledge.

♥ He who gets wisdom loves his own soul; he who keeps understanding will find good. (PROVERBS 19:8 NKJV)

♥ Whoever gives heed to instruction prospers, and blessed is the one who trusts in the LORD. (PROVERBS 16:20 NIV)

♥ The heart of the discerning acquires knowledge; for the ears of the wise seek it out. (PROVERBS 18:15 NIV)

Paige's Story: A Girl with HIV

Paige was born HIV positive. Overhearing a conversation between her mother and the doctor when she was twelve, she asked her mom about her diagnosis. Her mother explained that Paige was born HIV positive but did not have AIDS. She told her best friend, who didn't seem to have much of a reaction. . .but within days, everyone in her middle school was spreading rumors about it. In a crushing descent, she went from being very popular to having no friends at all. Kids at school called her PAIDS, and someone tacked a note on her locker that said, "No AIDS at this school!"

Isolated as sick and untouchable in the seventh grade, Paige began having stress-induced seizures. She sought help from the school counselor, who suggested she tell people it wasn't true.

But the bullying only escalated, and it became clear to Paige and her mother that the school administrators were not going to protect her. Determined and brave, Paige insisted on living a life of truth. A dancer, cheerleader, and athlete, she tried out for the soccer team in the eighth grade. After a game, her coach asked if it was true that she had AIDS.

"No," Paige replied, because she was HIV positive—and that doesn't mean a person has AIDS.

The coach joked to her mother, saying, "Well, if we keep you on the team, it could work to our advantage because the other players won't want to touch you, and you could score goals."

- ♡ Every nine and a half minutes someone in the United States contracts HIV.

- ♡ Nearly one in six peple who are infected with HIV are unaware of their infection.

- ♡ An estimated one in four new HIV infections happens among youth ages thirteen to twenty-four.

- ♡ More than 1.1 million people in the United States are living with HIV, and fifty thousand new cases are reported each year.

I Need You to Listen, Hear, and Understand Me

Paige left her middle school, and while being home-schooled, she decided to take a stand. She began speaking out and sharing her story. At the age of fourteen, Paige was granted special permission to become the youngest person ever certified through the American Red Cross as an HIV/AIDS educator. She even pleaded to Congress and helped pass an antibullying bill in 2013. She found a new high school where she was accepted and applauded for standing up and speaking out. All through high school, Paige was the guest speaker for the "I Need You to Listen, Hear, and Understand Me" Tour. She became a nationwide ambassador for bullying and HIV/AIDS. She has been named in the Top 10 Young Women to Watch list, and when she graduated from high school, she was chosen by the faculty to receive the Outstanding Leadership Award and named by her fellow students as Most Likely to Change the World.[1]

---

1. To learn more about how Paige is impacting the world for good, go to PaigeRawl.com.

The Real Dish on STDs

So here's the real dish, the skinny-minny, me and you, over coffee: STDs are transmitted by sharing bodily fluids: blood, semen, vaginal fluids, and breast milk. Think fluids, think body. They are not spread through hugging, touching, or soccer games. It's got to be blood on blood; semen (the fluid that comes out of the male sex organ) on vagina (the female sex organ). It can spread through two men having sex, two women, or heterosexual sex, which is male-female. It can be passed through sharing needles in intravenous drug use, which is injecting illegal drugs into the veins. Tattoo parlors can also inadvertently spread infection by using dirty needles—so extra precaution needs to be taken there. In the old days, STDs could be passed through blood transfusions, but hospitals test for that now and most medical care in developed countries can be trusted in that area—but it never hurts to ask should you need a blood transfusion. Finally, STDs can be passed to babies through childbirth or breastfeeding.

STDs can, but not always, be an unfortunate consequence of sexual immorality. (Remember, Paige contracted AIDS through childbirth, through no fault

How is HIV spread?

Through four bodily fluids only:

♥ blood

♥ semen

♥ vaginal fluids

♥ breast milk

of her own.) STDs can happen to good girls in good families with good friends and good intentions.

STDs can happen in marriage if one of the partners has had sex with other people. They are vicious viruses and bacterial infections that *you really want to live your whole life without.* In fact, I would venture to say you would be quite pleased to avoid them altogether—to never ever have to deal with the effects of an STD—and anyone who has one would agree.

Here's a major consequence of STDs: when left untreated, they can mess with a woman's reproductive system, as they did in Boo's case. They can be passed to one's spouse. And

STD are common among young people.[1]

♡ Half of new cases reported every year are among people ages fifteen to twenty-four.

♡ One out of four teenage girls has an STD.

there's this weird shame thing that comes along with them, too—like, "I'm gross because I have these warts or this virus and I have to deal with it now; I'm dirty; don't touch me"—when in truth, everyone wants to be touched and held. So there are *emotional* consequences to STDS, too.[3]

Let's just remember, there's not a virus on earth that can make a person gross. He or she may feel gross, but the virus does not make them gross. They have contracted a disease, and it needs to be treated.

2. Facts from WebMD, "Understanding Sexually Trandmitted Disease," and girlshealth.gov, "What are STDs and STIs?"
3. These emotions are best processed with someone who understands the repercussions of sexually transmitted diseases, like a Christian counselor.

What are the consequences of STDS?

STDs can have long-term consequences:

♥ These include problems with your reproductive system, like not being able to have children.

♥ They include, pain, cancer, and permanent damage to your body.

♥ Some STDs, like HIV, cannot be cured and can be deadly.

What Are STDs and How Do You Get Them?[4]

♥ STDs are sexually transmitted diseases (also called STIs, sexually transmitted infections).

♥ You can get an STD by having sexual contact with someone who already has an STD.

♥ You can get an STD through sexual intercourse or by putting your mouth, hands, or genitals on the genitals or on the sores of someone who is infected.

---

4. Information was gathered from: "What Are STDs and STIs?" GirlsHealth.gov, November 25, 2015, http://www.girlshealth.gov /sexuality/sti.html; "Understanding Sexually Transmitted Diseases (STDs)," WebMD, February 7, 2015, http://www.webmd.com/sex-relationships /understanding-stds-basics; and "Facts You Should Know about Sexually Transmitted Diseases and Staying Healthy," Danya International, Inc., June 18, 2003, http://www.stopthinkbesafe.org/stdFacts/stdFact.asp. For fact sheets on each STD, go to: "Sexually Transmitted Diseases (STDs)" Centers for Disease Control and Prevention, January 14, 2016, http://www.cdc.gov/std/healthcomm/fact_sheets.htm.

💛 STDs are highly contagious—they spread very easily.

💛 STDs are caused by various bacteria and viruses—and even tiny insects.

What Are the Symptoms of STDs?

Most people with STDs have *no symptoms*.

If symptoms do appear, they can be tricky. It is possible for them to show up anywhere from two days to a few months or even several years after contracting an STD. Symptoms might include:

💛 bumps or blisters near the mouth or genitals

💛 burning or pain during urination or a bowel movement

💛 flulike symptoms, including fever, chills, aches, and swelling in the groin area

💛 stomach pain

💛 fluid coming out of the vagina that is yellow, gray, or green, or has a strong smell

If you have one of these symptoms or suspect you may have contracted an STD, contact your doctor immediately. Better to find out now and treat it than to carry the infection and not know it.

If you've had sex even once, you must see your doctor to find out which STD tests you may need.

Be brave. Face the situation and take care of yourself and your potential future husband, and save yourself the heartache of possibly harming yourself for life.

Can STDs Be Treated?

Some STDs can be treated and cured, but not all of them.

Even if you get treated, you can get the STD again if you continue to have sex. There are two categories of STDs: bacterial and viral.[5]

♡ Bacterial STDs, such as gonorrhea, syphilis, and chlamydia, are cured with antibiotics *if diagnosed early on and treated quickly.* If not, these STDS can cause permanent damage to your reproductive system and your body overall. If left unchecked, they can also be passed to your children during childbirth.

♡ Viral STDs, such as HIV, HPV (which causes genital warts), herpes, and hepatitis B (the only STD that can be prevented with a vaccine)—the "four Hs"—have no cure, but their symptoms can be reduced with treatment.

There are vaccines that can help prevent two STDs:

♡ The hepatitis B vaccine (usually given at birth)

♡ The HPV vaccine, which guards against genital warts and cervical cancer (this is often given in the teenage years—ask your doctor if you've had the vaccine).

As with any vaccine, educate yourself on the potential risks and dangers.

How Can I Keep from Getting an STD?

The surest way to avoid getting an STD is not to have sexual intercourse and other kinds of intimate sexual contact. Stay away from drugs and alcohol, which can lead to having unsafe sex. Except for abstinence (not having sex), condoms made

5. See a list of definitions, symptoms, and treatment options for STDs in the next chapter.

from latex and coated with a proper lubricant are the best protection against STDs. A condom is a thin protective latex covering for the penis so that when a man ejaculates, the sperm are caught inside the condom. When used consistently and correctly, condoms can reduce one's risk of contracting STDs, but they do not provide 100 percent protection. Keep in mind they work better at preventing some STDs than others. Still, if a girl chooses to have sex, she should make sure to use a condom. Around eighteen out of one hundred women who use a male condom over the course of a year may still get pregnant.[6] So don't be fooled; they are beneficial but *not 100 percent effective.*

If you do have sex, you'll be safer if:

♥ Both you and your partner got tested for STDs (and treated if necessary).

♥ The two of you only have sex with each other.

♥ You always use a latex condom (and use it correctly).

♥ Abstinence (waiting to have sex until marriage) is the best and safest choice.

How Can I Know If I Have an STD?

The only way to know if a person has an STD is to be tested. Remember, lots of infections have no symptoms, especially in the early stages. By the time symptoms do show up, the infection may already have done damage.

Sometimes people are too scared or embarrassed to ask for STD information or testing. But many STDs are easy to

6. For more information about birth control options, go to "Types of Birth Control," GirlsHealth.gov, May 28, 2014, http://girlshealth.gov/body/sexuality/bc_types.html.

treat—and dangerous if they're not treated.

Here's what to expect when getting checked for an STD:

💟 The doctor will examine your skin, throat, and genital area for sores, growths, and rashes. He or she may also look inside your vagina and at your cervix.[7]

💟 Your doctor may take a sample to test from:

Fluid or tissue from your genital, vaginal, or anal areas

Blood

Urine (pee)

These tests are usually quick and painless.

💟 When the doctor gets the results, he or she will let you know if you have an STD and what to do take care of your health. Sometimes your doctor may want to treat you even before you get your test results. Follow up to get the results and any other care you need. (It is important to see your doctor regularly.)

Those who choose to have sex should make sure the person they are having sex with is also seeing a doctor. Remember people contract STDs through sex—so both people need to be tested, treated, and held accountable for their sexual choices.

If you find out you have an STD, it is your responsibility to notify the people you have had sex with so they can seek treatment as well.

Again, be brave. Be real. And do the right thing. It would devastate you to find out later that you had given someone an STD that was, let's say, passed on to his wife, who then could no longer bear children.

It's a domino effect—one person passes it to another, to another. So remove yourself from the lineup.

---

7. *Cervix* (say: *SUR-viks*) is the narrow entryway between the vagina and the uterus. The muscles of the cervix are flexible so that it can expand to let a baby pass through when he or she is being born.

Privacy, Please.

Last, I'd like to mention something that Paige, our girl-born-with-HIV, may agree with. If someone confides in you their honest-to-goodness, not-so-pretty truth about having an STD, keep it to yourself. It is up to that person to take responsibility for her choices and inform the people it affects. There is nothing worse than a friend who gossips about you, heaping shame upon shame. It's hard enough to deal with an STD; the last thing a girl needs is rumors or condemnation about it.

True friends cover each other's stories. And, remember, a girl's story is hers alone to tell. So, no rocks. No blame. As the Word says, "He who conceals a transgression seeks love, but he who repeats a matter separates intimate friends" (Proverbs 17:9 NASB). My best friend, Trish, always said to me, "You know I'm a vault, Jen. You can tell me anything and I won't tell a soul, unless you need help." I always knew that to be true, and that's why I consider her one of my best friends to this day. Trish always told me the truth and directed me in the way I should go. If I was doing something that was hurting me, she told me straight to my face. She never gossiped about me behind my back. She is a true friend; she is up front and honest with me, and leaves it up to me to make the changes I need to make.

So if you or a friend ever get an STD, tell each other the truth. They are not shameful; they are contagious. You have to stop having sex, tell whoever has been involved in your sexual escapades, get your rear end to the doctor (literally!), and see what can be done about it.

And if it's not about you but about a friend who confides in you, tell her the truth, and remember Paige. You may need to be her vault, a safe place to land when times get tough.

MYTH 13:

STDs Won't Happen to Me.
(As long as we use "protection.")

—

TRUTH 13:

It *Can* Happen to You!
(So let's get educated.)

LIFE VERSE:

No temptation has overtaken you that is not common to man. God is faithful, and he will not let you be tempted beyond your ability, but with the temptation he will also provide the way of escape, that you may be able to endure it.

1 CORINTHIANS 10:13 ESV

Contagious, Contagious, Contagious

You sneeze, you wipe your hands on a rag, and another person comes up and wipes her hands on the rag, then rubs her eyes. *Voila!* You have now passed your cold on to someone else. You chug a water bottle after someone who has a sore throat has already taken a drink, and you wake up the next day with a sore throat. You take in the breath of someone who has the flu, and guess what? You have the flu. People are passing around bacteria and viruses because they are sharing the same towels, cups, and air.

People are passing around STDs because they are sharing the same beds (not having a harmless girls' sleepover; they are sleeping *together—their bodies are on top of each other in all kinds of positions*). People who have sores on their mouths are kissing people who have no sores. Then their mouths are touching each other's genitals. Then their genitals are touching other people's genitals who previously had no viruses. Then their infected genitals are penetrating the uninfected genitals of another person. At this point, your mouth, your bodily fluids, and your genitals have virtually been touched, kissed, and penetrated by the diseases of a bunch of other people. Get it?

Good. I'm glad you got it. Now, can we recognize why God said this was *not good*?

The best form of protection against STDs is to *not engage in sexual intimacy* with

♥ someone who is not your marriage partner

♥ someone who has not been tested

♥ someone who has been sharing his bodily fluids, hands, mouth, and genitals with other people

It doesn't take a PhD to understand it.

But here's the striking truth: young people are *not* getting it. Half of new cases reported every year are among teens and early twentysomethings. One in four teenage girls has an STD.

Education is key. So let's test your knowledge of STDs. Just like you know what poison ivy, chicken pox, bronchitis, and the flu are, let's see if you know the difference between HPV, HIV, chlamydia, and genital herpes.

And yes, there will be a test at the end. So take notes. Highlight. Underline. Mark with an X the things you don't want, and circle the ones you do.

Most Common STDs

There are more than twenty-five STDs caused by many different bacteria and viruses. One partner can expose you to many diseases. You are at risk of getting all the STDs that your partner's past and present partners have had.

Here is a list of the most common STDs, including definitions, symptoms, and treatment.[1]

- Chlamydia:

  ♥ **What is it?** Chlamydia is a very common STD. Women who have it are much more likely to get HIV if they have been exposed to it.

  ♥ If it's not treated, chlamydia can cause serious problems, like pelvic inflammatory disease and not being able to have children.

---

1. For more detailed explanations of each STD, see "Types of STDs (STIs)," GirlsHealth.gov, November 15, 2015, http://girlshealth.gov /body/sexuality/symptoms.html.

♡ **What are some symptoms?** Often none. Could cause: unusual vaginal discharge, pain, nausea, fever, pain during sex, bleeding between periods.

♡ **How is it treated?** Chlamydia can be cured with antibiotics if detected early.

- Genital Herpes:

    ♡ **What is it?** Genital herpes is caused by a virus called herpes simplex virus (HSV).

    ♡ There are two types of herpes virus that cause genital herpes: HSV-1 and HSV-2. A person with HSV-1—which is oral herpes, or cold sores around a person's mouth—can pass the virus to another person's genitals during oral sex.

    ♡ Genital herpes can increase the risk of HIV infection. That's because HIV can enter the body more easily where there's a break in the skin, such as a herpes sore.

    ♡ **What are some symptoms?** Sometimes none. May cause red bumps, blisters, or open sores in the genital area or anus (bottom) that can hurt very badly. May also cause fever, headache, muscle aches, swollen genitals, itching or burning in the genital area, and pain in the legs, buttocks, or genital area or while urinating.

    ♡ **How is it treated?** There is no cure, but medicine can help make the breakouts shorter and less frequent. Even if you're taking medicine, you can spread herpes when you have sores. Even if you have no sores, there's still a chance of passing on the disease.

- Gonorrhea:

    ♡ **What is it?** Gonorrhea is a common STD that has become more difficult to treat successfully because germs have built up resistance to medicine.

♡ Having gonorrhea can make you more likely to get HIV if you're exposed to it. Untreated gonorrhea can cause serious problems like not being able to get pregnant.

♡ This STD can also spread to the blood, joints, heart, or even the brain.

♡ Any young person who has had sex should be tested for gonorrhea.

♡ What are some symptoms? Most often, none. Can include: yellow, green, or smelly vaginal discharge; burning when peeing; pain during sex; bleeding between periods.

♡ Gonorrhea infection can also be present in the throat, which may cause a sore throat. It can also spread to the eyes, causing pain and sensitivity to light.

♡ It can also be present in the anus. Symptoms are anal discharge, anal itching, soreness, bleeding, painful bowl movements.

♡ **How is it treated?** Gonorrhea can be cured with antibiotics, but some cases are harder to treat.

• Hepatitis B:

♡ **What is it?** Hepatitis B (HBV) is caused by a virus that attacks the liver. If it doesn't go away, it can lead to *liver cancer* and other *serious liver problems.*

   • Most babies in the United States now get vaccinated for HBV. Talk to your doctor and look at your health records to see if you have been vaccinated.

   • Ask your doctor about testing if you or your parents were born in a country where HBV is common, such as countries in Africa and Asia.

   • If you live with someone who has HBV, you are at risk and should be tested.

♡ **What are some symptoms?** Often none. Could cause yellow skin or yellowing of the whites of the eyes, tiredness, dark-colored urine, stomach pain, loss of appetite, nausea and vomiting, diarrhea, low fever, headache or muscle aches, hives or skin rash, joint pain and swelling. Symptoms usually appear six to twelve weeks after infection.

♡ Warning: you can contract HBV if an infected person's blood, semen, or other bodily fluid enters your body. It can also happen if you:

- *share drug needles with an infected person*

- *get a tattoo or piercing using a needle with the virus on it*

- *use an infected person's toothbrush or razor*

♡ **How is it treated?** There is no cure for hepatitis B. Often, it goes away without treatment, but some young people develop lifelong problems from it. It can be treated with certain medicines that can help slow down the infection. These medicines are not safe for pregnant women. See your doctor if you have recently been exposed to the virus. You may be able to get treatment to lower the risk of coming down with the disease.

- HIV/AIDS:

  ♡ **What is it?** Human immunodeficiency virus, or HIV, is the virus that can cause AIDS (acquired immunodeficiency syndrome). Unlike some other viruses, the human body cannot get rid of HIV. That means that once you have HIV, you have it for life.

  ♡ How does HIV lead to AIDS?

  - HIV weakens the body's ability to fight infections and diseases by attacking specific cells of the immune system, called CD4 or T cells. Over time, HIV can destroy so many of these cells that the body can't fight off infection and disease. When this happens, HIV can lead to AIDS.[2]

- AIDS is the stage of infection that occurs when the immune system is badly damaged and becomes vulnerable to infections and cancers. When the number of CD4 cells falls too low, the person has progressed to AIDS. Without

HIV Facts for Youth[3]

♡ About 60 percent of all youth with HIV do not know they are infected, are not getting treated, and can unknowingly pass the virus on to others.

♡ One in four new HIV infections occurs in youth ages thirteen to twenty-four years.

♡ About one thousand youth per month in the United States are infected with HIV.

♡ The greatest number of infections occurs among gay and bisexual youth.

♡ Nearly half of all new infections among youth occur in African-American males.

♡ The risk for HIV for most youth begins when they start having sex or start injecting drugs.

♡ HIV causes a serious infection that, without treatment, leads to AIDS and early death.

---

2. Information gathered from: "HIV Among Youth in the US," Centers for Disease Control and Prevention, January 8, 2013, http://www.cdc.gov/vitalsigns/hivamongyouth/; "What Are STDs and STIs?", GirlsHealth.gov, November 25, 2015, girlshealth.gov/body/sexuality/sti.html; and "About HIV and AIDS," Centers for Disease Control and Prevention, December 6, 2015, http://www.cdc.gov/hiv/basics/whatishiv.html.

treatment, people with AIDS typically survive about one to three years. People with AIDS need medical treatment to prevent death.

♥ **Can you die from HIV/AIDS?** Yes. It used to be that almost everyone diagnosed with AIDS died. Great progress has been made in diagnosing and treating the disease and extending life expectancy. But HIV continues to be a serious health issue in the world.

- Worldwide: Almost 37 million people are living with HIV around the world. There are about 2 million new cases of HIV a year. Over 1 million people die from AIDS-related illnesses each year, and about 39 million people worldwide have died of AIDS-related causes since the epidemic began. Seventy percent of all people who have HIV are living in Africa.

- In the United States: Over a million people in the United States are living with HIV, and about 13 percent don't know they are infected. Each year, fifty thousand new cases are reported, half of them being young people. Almost fifteen thousand people die each year from HIV-related illnesses, and seven hundred thousand people in the United States have died from it since the epidemic began.[3]

♥ **What are some symptoms?** Women and girls with HIV may have no symptoms for years. Even if HIV causes no symptoms, it is still causing problems with your immune system that need treatment as early as possible.

- Some people have flulike symptoms within the first few weeks or months after getting infected with HIV.

- Symptoms of AIDS: weight loss; fever, chills and night sweats; fatigue; headache; diarrhea, vomiting, and nausea; mouth, genital, or anal sores; dry cough; rash; swollen lymph

3. "HIV/AIDS, Basic Statistics," Centers for Disease Control and Prevention, November 3, 2015, http://www.cdc.gov/hiv/basics/statistics.html.

nodes; other STDs; vaginal infections; pelvic inflammatory disease (see below) that does not get better with treatment; menstrual cycle changes, like not having periods; human papillomavirus (HPV—see text that follows), which can cause genital warts and cervical cancer.

♡ **How could you get it?** You can get infected with HIV from blood, semen, pre-semen (fluids from the penis before ejaculation), vaginal fluid, and anal mucus (fluids in your bottom).

- This can happen during oral, anal, or vaginal sex. It can also happen when these fluids get into an open wound or sore.

- You also can get HIV from sharing needles for drugs, tattoos, or piercings with an infected person.

- You can't get HIV from casual contact, like sneezing or touching.

♡ You cannot rely on symptoms to know whether you have HIV.

♡ More than half of young people with HIV do not know they have it.

♡ The only way to know for sure is to be tested.

♡ **How is it treated?** There is no cure for HIV, but there are treatments that help infected people live longer and healthier lives. Antiretroviral therapy (ART) can dramatically prolong the lives of many people infected with HIV and lower their chances of infecting others. It's important that people get tested early, know they are infected, and get medical care.[4]

---

4. For more information on HIV/AIDS testing, treatment, and prevention, go to the CDC's site for HIV/AIDS at http://www.cdc.gov/hiv/. For information specific to HIV among youth, go to http://www.cdc.gov/vitalsigns/HIVAmongYouth.

♡ How can you avoid getting HIV/AIDS?

- Get the facts and understand your risk.

- Talk with parents, doctors, and other trusted adults about HIV, sexual health, and concerns about depression, drugs, or alcohol.

- Resist pressure to have sex or inject drugs. Do not pressure others to engage in risky behaviors.

- If you are sexually active, stop having sex. Do not have sex with an older person who may be more likely to already have HIV. If you insist on having sex, use a condom every time—but remember condoms are not 100 percent effective.

What Puts You at Risk for HIV?

♡ Having sex

♡ Injecting drugs

♡ Having sex under the influence of drugs or alcohol

♡ Living in communities where a higher percentage of people already have HIV

♡ African-Americans have a greater burden of HIV than any other racial or ethnic group.

♡ Gay and bisexual men are forty times more likely to have HIV than other men (fewer than half of gay and bisexual males in high school used condoms that last time they had sex).

♡ Having sex with men who are gay or bisexual

More HIV Facts

♥ About 87 percent of young males got HIV from male-to-male sex, 6 percent from heterosexual sex, 2 percent from injection drug use, and about 5 percent from a combination of male-to-male sex and injection drug use.

♥ About 86 percent of young females got HIV through heterosexual sex and 13 percent from injection drug use.

♥ Young men are far more likely than young women to have HIV and are also less likely to get tested.

• Human Papillomavirus (HPV)

♥ **What is it?** Human papillomavirus, or HPV, is the most common STD in the United States. While it often goes away on its own, some types of HPV can cause genital warts, cervical cancer, and other types of cancer.

> • The HPV vaccine can help prevent cervical cancer and genital warts. Ask your doctor and parents about getting vaccinated, and be sure to research the potential risks and side effects.

♥ **What are some symptoms?** Some people have none. They can include warts on the genitals, inner thighs, and anus that cause itching, burning, and pain; or growths on the cervix and vagina that can't be seen.

♥ **How is it treated?** There is no treatment for HPV. However, there are treatments for the conditions that it can cause, like genital warts and cervical cell changes. Warts can be removed through special medications or minor surgery.

- Pubic Lice

    ♡ **What is it?** Lice (a kind of tiny insect) that feeds on human blood. Also known as "crabs." It can be transmitted by skin-to-skin contact with someone who already has it.

    ♡ **What are the symptoms?** Itching in the pubic area; finding lice or eggs attached to your pubic hair; sores from bites or scratching; rust-colored spots on your underwear; mild fever and tiredness if you've been bitten by a large number of lice.

    ♡ **How is it treated?** A prescription or over-the-counter medication can kill the adult lice and egg lice. You must wash any sheets and clothing that could have lice in them, and as with any STD, avoid any sexual contact until the treatment is complete.

- Syphilis

    ♡ **What is it?** Syphilis that is not treated can lead to serious problems and even death. Also, the sores caused by syphilis make it easier to get or give someone HIV during sex.

    ♡ **What are some symptoms?** An infected person may not have any symptoms for years, but he or she can still give the disease to someone else.

    Different stages have different symptoms.

        - Symptoms in the first stage appear ten to ninety days after getting infected. They include a painless sore, usually in the genital area, but possibly on the lips or other parts of the body that had contact with a syphilis sore from another person.

        - Sores heal on their own in three to six weeks. If the infection is not treated, a secondary stage follows. Symptoms include: a rash on the palms and soles of the feet that doesn't itch and goes away on its own; fever; swollen lymph glands and sore throat;

patchy hair loss; raised gray, warty-looking areas in moist places, such as the genital area, armpits, and anus (bottom); headaches and muscle aches; weight loss; tiredness.

- If the infection is still not treated, it moves to a hidden stage. Then it can possibly enter a last stage when there is damage to the brain, nerves, eyes, heart, and blood vessels. Some people may even die.

♡ **How is it treated?** If it is diagnosed and treated early, syphilis can be cured with antibiotics.

- Trichomoniasis

♡ **What is it?** Trichomoniasis is *very common* in sexually active young women. It is transmitted through vaginal sex or skin-to-skin genital contact with no penetration. Sometimes called "trich," it is caused by a parasite (a tiny organism that feeds off you). Having trichomoniasis increases your chances of getting HIV if you're exposed to it.

♡ **What are the symptoms?** Some women don't have symptoms, but those who do can have symptoms appear between five to twenty-eight days after getting infected. Symptoms can include: foamy yellow-green vaginal discharge with a strong odor; discomfort during sex and when urinating; irritation and itching of the genital area; lower abdominal pain.

♡ **How is it treated?** It usually can be cured with antibiotics. Whoever you have had sex with should be treated as well.

- Pelvic Inflammatory Disease

♡ **What is it?** Pelvic inflammatory disease (PID) is not an STD, but it is a serious infection in your reproductive system that you can get from some STDs. PID can lead to problems like ongoing pain in the pelvic area and not being able to have a baby.

- Teen girls and young women who have sex are most at risk for PID because they have a cervix that is still developing. This increases the chances of getting STDs that lead to PID. The more sex partners a person has, the greater the chances of getting it, too.

♡ **How do you avoid getting PID?** If you want to avoid getting STDs, your best bet is not having sex. Condoms can reduce the chance of getting STDs that can lead to PID, but they have to be used the right way every time and are not fail-proof. If you are having sex, make sure to see your doctor and get tested for STDs. Early treatment is critical.

Wise Instructions

♡ "Because of the temptation to sexual immorality, each man should have his own wife and each woman her own husband." (1 CORINTHIANS 7:2 ESV)

♡ "'Therefore a man shall leave his father and mother and hold fast to his wife, and the two shall become one flesh.' . . .What therefore God has joined together, let not man separate." (MATTHEW 19:5–6)

In God We Trust

After our very important, very long list of sexually transmitted diseases, we can understand why God's Word teaches us to flee from sexual promiscuity and advises us to cleave to one person for life.

Maybe from the beginning God had a plan for safe sex. His Word serves as a loving protection and guard around us. When He gives us this instruction, He means it for our good.

The bottom-line truth is that STDs can happen to you. And God can redeem even that, just as He did for Boo through her amazing adoption story. He can take the painful trials of life, the path we didn't want to take, and transform the broken stones into a walkway of victory. He's an expert at that.

But He would never give us instruction that wasn't possible for us. Sexual temptation is powerful, but it can be resisted, and He will always give us a doorway out of the burning building or a stairwell we can run down to safety.

We certainly have the power to resist sexual sin in marriage. So why wouldn't we resist it while we are unmarried?

MYTH 14:

Homosexual, Bisexual, and Transgender People Are Sinful.

(The real question is, are they born that way?)

—

TRUTH 14:

People Who Struggle with Their Sexuality Need Love.

(And you can be the one to give it to them.)

LIFE VERSE:

In passing judgment on another you condemn yourself. . .not knowing that God's kindness is meant to lead you to repentance. . . . For all have sinned and fall short of the glory of God, and are justified by his grace as a gift.

ROMANS 2:1, 4, 3:23–24 ESV

Fear and Faith

There are moments in my life when I have been totally controlled by fear. If the steering wheel of my car could tell stories of the times I've gripped it tightly and begged for deliverance from anxiety, you could hardly bear the drama. Or maybe you'd understand because you've been there yourself. Do you fear the unknown? Do you ever fear for the future, a humongous black question mark, wishing greatly that for just one moment you could know what's coming? I have.

I felt this way about this chapter. I avoided writing it. I didn't want to face something that looks like a big black hole on the landscape of our lives, tiptoeing around it for fear that I'd fall right into the abyss where so many people already are: judged or judging others for their approach to the lesbian, gay, bisexual, and transgender (LGBT) community. For they are a *community*. They are people; they are souls; they are not faceless, nameless enemies of the cross; they are the reason for the cross, just like we are; they are human beings handmade by God, for His glory, worthy of His blood and precious to Him.

Unfortunately, some Christians have deeply offended and condemned people in the LGBT community, and I will say it from the get-go: homophobia—the fear of or discrimination against homosexuals—is a sin. It is fear of what we do not know, what we cannot imagine, and what we don't understand. Over three hundred times in the Bible, God tells us not to fear. On the flip side of that coin, He tells us to fear one thing and one thing only, and that is Him.

As Caleb Kaltenbach, a pastor raised by two gay parents describes, homophobia is the fear of some people for whom Jesus died and to whom He sent us to share the gospel. This inordinate fear causes us to alienate ourselves from them and give up any chance of influencing them for Christ.

Homophobia is a form of spiritual discrimination, and we need to radically purge it from our midst.[1]

Sadly, the Christian community has done a shoddy job of loving the LGBT community. In many ways, we have failed to connect ourselves through our common interests, common struggles, and common goals—which is something Jesus modeled and Paul emphasized we must do to reach those who are different than us.[2] Both the Christian and LGBT community want to be heard, known, and respected for their beliefs; and both value acceptance, fellowship, and social justice. We also have these experiences in common: a desire to be good parents, serve our communities, have healthy relationships, be free from addictions, and experience peace.

As a whole, Christians have also failed to show the LGBT community the true Jesus: that Jesus Himself was a celibate man, rejected by men, hated, despised, accused, abandoned, tempted, humiliated, and scorned by His own flesh and blood—and that He of all people can identify with the pain many gay people know in their lifetimes. Jesus Himself knows what it is to have your heart crushed by hate.

And it is exactly that—the hatefulness; the mocking, abusing voices; the insults and condemnations toward gay people that drive them away from the saving grace of Jesus instead of drawing them toward it.

I'm going to use this white space I've been granted to publicly apologize to the LGBT community on behalf of Christ-followers for any way we have condemned, hurt, misunderstood, judged, or belittled you. Nowhere in the Gospels do I see my Jesus treating people this way. The only people He says are condemned are the religious ones who judge—and those who reject His invitation into the

1. Caleb Kaltenbach, *Messy Grace* (Colorado Springs, CO: Waterbrook, 2015), 169.
2. 1 Corinthians 9:19–23

freest life. I am so very sorry. On behalf of all of us, I ask forgiveness not only for the cruelty Christians have exacted on you, but the judgmental stares, the awkward silences, the condemning voices, and most of all, the alienation you have experienced from the church. In truth, the church should always have been an open door with the light on so that in your darkest hour, at any hour, you knew you were welcome there—and you knew that love was there: the living water, bread and wine, communion, friendship, compassion, and companionship—the kind of companionship Jesus offered to people marginalized by society. I'm sorry we haven't pursued you the way Jesus pursued people and offered you hope without expecting you to clean up first. I am extremely sorry for that—so I ask forgiveness for our behavior, but also for the *impact* of our behavior on your life—emotionally, mentally, physically, and spiritually.

On one very recent drive, I was parked at a stoplight, squeezing the life out of my poor steering wheel, crying and begging God to deliver me from anxiety. I have done this many, many times and yet still have been gripped by relentless fears. But there was something different this time. Right there, at the intersection by the junior high, with the neon lights of the donut shop on the left and the drugstore lit up on the right, I broke.

Now, I'm a girl who has broken and broken—who has surrendered and surrendered her battles to Jesus. My carpet knows my fists and my tears.

But this time something snapped, and I went home a different person that day.

Faith has replaced fear as my driver.

People can be set free from long-standing battles that are contrary to the best life described for us in scripture.

I'm stoked. One small benefit is that I became able to write this chapter.

Knowing and Loving Gay People

As a young woman, I sat in many a makeup chair with gay makeup artists and hairstylists doing me up for the current job—whether I was modeling for Eddie Bauer or Jordache Jeans, for Olay or Giorgio Armani, for bridal or fashion—gay and lesbian makeup artists, hair stylists, clothing stylists, designers, photographers, and models were simply a part of my world. There are many colorful threads of people in fashion photography, runway design, and television—and I never feared these people or thought there was anything to fear.

Hair stylists and women have an uncommon bond—as soon as the hairdresser starts touching your head, the two of you start sharing. And what I remember from the countless hours in those makeup chairs is this: many homosexual men struggle with rejection, relationships, and identity. I don't believe theirs is a road many would pick—because there seemed to be a lot of pain on that road.

Then again there's been a lot of pain on my road, too. And the number one most healing thing in the world for me has been love.

I like love that compliments. It's kind of funny, but I'm a sucker for a compliment. It just feels so good on the inside for someone to see what is good in me and call it out. I like love that pursues me, too—don't you? Love that seeks me out and finds me where I am and hugs me, holds me, wipes a tear away, shares a laugh, swaps a story. I just love it when someone seeks me out and finds me. I also like love that touches me. Give me a hug, please? Reach out and hold my hands and look into my eyes, put your hand on my shoulder or back, and show me like Jesus did that you aren't afraid to touch me when I'm messed up and having a hard time. Love never identifies me with my sin.

I remember one time I was speaking on TV, and the lady introduced me as a model who was anorexic and suicidal. I was so irritated as I sat down on live TV for that interview. I wanted her to introduce me as a conqueror: a wife, mother, forgiven and set free, an author of books and Bible studies—because those things are what I value the most. After that I took control over my introductions and wrote them *for* the hosts!

If you've been following my heart so far in this book, you also know I love grace. I love knowing that I am more than my struggles, more than my history, a victor over all things—even fear and anxiety, which have been following me around for thirty years or more. I love being around people who see past all that and just deposit Jesus' radical, grace-filled love. Those are the people who help me grow and who help me break free of the ties that have bound me. . .people who are willing to invest in a relationship with me, to speak love and truth in kindness and not in condemnation—for no one changes in the face of condemnation. It is always kindness that changes us.

My mentor, Devi Titus, is one of those rare women whose kindness has changed my life. Her husband calls her the Holy Spirit, if that is any indication of how she fills a room. Radiant and gentle, correcting but loving, Devi recently sat in my living room while the lights of Christmas twinkled behind her, paling in comparison to the bling in her eyes (and on her body—Devi is the queen of bling. When she first got into ministry in the 1970s, she was the only pastor's wife wearing a feather boa). I confessed all my troubles to her that day, my battles between fear and faith—and do you want to know what Devi did?

She reached out and touched me and confirmed that honesty is good. Because I was open to it, and because we have a long-standing relationship based on mutual respect, she pointed out some things that were out of order in my life and shared how I could get them back in alignment. When she left my house, she spoke the name of Jesus over my anxiety, and she held me in her arms with the softest touch imaginable, whispering, "Everything you want to hold on to, let go of." She backed up, turned her wrists upward with her palms toward me and fingers raised, saying, "Surrender."

It must have been just a few days later that I surrendered at the stoplight. Peace has been my governor ever since that day.

Love like that changes people. Love is our highest calling.

All those years I sat in the makeup chairs, I didn't know Jesus. If I could go back to those days, I'd linger longer. I'd listen more intently. Ask more questions. Leave surprise chocolates in the chair when I was gone, or tell them about the living water that fills our cups until they runneth over.

You know, Jesus told the story of the living water to a Samaritan woman—and in that day, Jews "didn't associate with Samaritans." Not only was she of the outcast group, but she also struggled with sexual sin. Jesus always looked past the cultural issues, sought the outcast, pursued the broken, and offered free healing. He engaged with messed-up people.

I have a dear friend who is gay whom I care for deeply. As long as she can remember, she has dreamed of marrying a woman. She is near and dear to my heart, and if anyone tried to bash her, I'd stand right there in the middle between them. Bash me, but don't bash the already bruised. She has lived a hard life, and she is a survivor. There is so much hope for her.

But my calling in her life is not to convince her she shouldn't be gay. My calling in her life is to love her as Christ loves me. Right there in the tension between grace and truth, we find the way.

Caleb's Story

Caleb's parents divorced when he was a toddler. His mother quickly proclaimed herself a lesbian and lived with her monogamous partner for twenty-two years. They took Caleb to many LGBT parties and gay pride parades, and Caleb experienced firsthand the hatred of some Christians toward gay people. His father was also a gay man who didn't tell Caleb about his sexuality until after Caleb graduated from college.

Caleb grew up hating Christians for their insults against his mother and father, whom he loved. But Jesus kept knocking on the door of Caleb's heart, through a note passed by a girl in school, through friends, and finally through a youth event in which he gave his life to Christ.

Now what was Caleb going to do? He had two gay parents. Would he side with grace or with truth? Grace says there is forgiveness for us all, that we all have access to God's throne through the blood of Christ. But truth says homosexuality is not God's created design for sexual intimacy. What now?

Caleb found a way to live in the tension of grace and truth. He left a church where he was preaching when he found out his mother and her partner were not welcome there—he stood up for grace. He attended the Talbot School of Theology and is completing a doctorate of ministry at

Dallas Theological Seminary. The man has studied the Word on this topic—and he knows what it says: the Bible is clear that sexual intimacy is designed to be experienced between one man and one woman.

But guess what? That didn't stop him from loving his parents and having a strong relationship with them. And when his mother moved to Dallas after her lifetime partner had died, people from his church personally moved her into her new apartment. They did the same for his father when he moved to Dallas, too. In fact, Caleb says his church did a better job of loving his parents than he did. They invited them to potlucks and barbecues, to join study groups, and to serve in the church, and showed even Caleb what love with skin on looks like.

Eventually, Caleb's parents both gave their lives to the Lord. In his astonishing, must-read book, *Messy Grace*, Caleb shares how love meets grace and walks in truth, and how it can get awfully messy at times. But Jesus came for messy people. Yep, He did. Like you. Like me. And like the people of the LGBT community.

I cried while reading Caleb's book, mostly at the end. And you know what made me cry? It was not learning that his parents finally surrendered to Christ—although that is miraculous and beautiful. It was at the point in the story that his mother's partner died that I cried, because she refused Jesus till her deathbed as far as Caleb saw, and Caleb was so heartbroken and crushed that he couldn't save her. The most painful part of his story was the notion that her anger against Christians, her bitterness and hardness toward the Gospel message may have prevented her from falling into the arms of Christ.

Gay, lesbian, bisexual, and transgender people have a place in God's kingdom—and it's right next to you and me.

I can say this while still believing the Bible teaches sexual intimacy that is blessed by God is in the context of one man and one woman in marriage. I can say this while also knowing that people in the LGBT community need another place of community—a place where they are pursued, embraced, and loved like Jesus loves—and that should be a community of believers!

Getting Messy

Sometimes we are so afraid of what we don't understand—of what's going to happen if we put ourselves out there—of what we cannot see. I get this. And I think Christians are afraid of gay pride parades. They fear transgender people. They don't know what to do about their relative or friend who is gay or bisexual. So we grasp tight on the steering wheel for control, and no matter how hard we squeeze, we can't fix the thing we don't understand. In my mind, God is saying to let go of trying to change people and to love them wholeheartedly, from the heart. Look past a person's struggles and offer them—right in the middle of their mess—the free gift of life.

Grace is a free gift, and once we truly receive grace, we can truly give it away.

Loving people who are living contrary to our beliefs can be very hard—alcoholics, convicts, abortion doctors, hypocrites, the sexually immoral—anyone who is living at the opposite end of the spectrum than us.[3] But let's remember: "While we were still sinners, Christ died for us" (Romans 5:8 ESV).

Not when we got cleaned up. Not when we became

---

3. Kaltenbach, *Messy Grace*, 31.

good. When we were in our sin, He died for us. So it's imperative, Caleb says, to have grace for people while they are still thinking and acting in ways that we might not agree with. Unless we choose to get involved in their lives in a loving way, they may never know how much God loves them.[4]

If you are a Christian, you should know the passage from 1 John 4, which tells us that "anyone who does not love does not know God, because God is love" (1 John 4:8 ESV).

So it's not homosexual people we should fear; it's ourselves. If we do not love, we do not know God. Loving is His signature characteristic of the true disciple.

> This is love: not that we loved God, but that he loved us and sent his Son as an atoning sacrifice for our sins. Dear friends, since God so loved us, we also ought to love one another. (1 John 4:10–11 NIV)

One time, after being confronted by a group of angry so-called "Christians," Caleb was upset and concerned for his mother. She told him not to worry and that she would be okay. She said she was glad she wasn't like other people who let themselves be controlled by hate.[5]

Let's not be controlled by hate.

Let's let go of the steering wheel, raise our palms, and let love be our guide.

The good news is, years later, Caleb's church used their hands and feet and hearts and homes to surround his mother with love, affection, and care, and then one day, after all those moments, she stepped into Jesus.

---

4. Ibid., 31–32.
5. Ibid., 40.

Is Homosexuality a Sin?

Sexual temptation is just that—temptation. For example, a person can be tempted to masturbate or look at pornography or engage in sexual activity outside of marriage and *choose not to*. Same-sex attraction is a temptation, not a sin. Everyone is tempted; it's whether or not we act on the temptation that makes it sin or not.

So are homosexual relations a sin? Let's remember that the word *sin* means "missing the mark." As much as we want to live in the grace boat and never have to get out, the answer is yes, it is a sin—homosexuality is missing the mark. From Genesis to Revelation, the Bible is consistent in upholding God's boundaries for sexual intimacy as between men and women. His boundaries are there to protect us, not isolate us. His boundaries are loving and good.

I believe Christians have elevated homosexual relations over other sins, and I think that's wrong.

For example, many people think God destroyed Sodom and Gomorrah because of the sin of homosexuality. But that's just one of the sins that ticked our Maker off—in actuality He destroyed them because of *arrogance*. He called them *"overfed and unconcerned"* and said they "did not help the poor and needy. They were haughty and did detestable things before me. Therefore I did away with them" (Ezekiel 16:49–50 NIV). The men of Sodom were seeking to have sex with Lot's visitors (who were actually angels disguised as men)—and Lot denied their request, saying it was "wicked." But then Lot did something just as disgusting: he offered up his virgin daughters to have sex with the men of Sodom. So the whole community was in sin, from being prideful to ignoring the poor to being sexually immoral.[6]

---

6. The information from this passage was taken from Kaltenbach, *Messy Grace*, 84–85.

If you want to live in the tension between grace and truth, you should know what the Bible says about homosexuality. I want you to study it for yourself, but here are some Old Testament verses about homosexuality:

♡ *"'Do not have sexual relations with a man as one does with a woman; that is detestable.'" (Leviticus 18:22 NIV)*

♡ *"'If a man has sexual relations with a man as one does with a woman, both of them have done what is detestable.'" (Leviticus 20:13 NIV)*

Now, some of the Old Testament law was superrandom and doesn't hold up today. For example, we are forbidden from eating shellfish in the Old Testament law. But Jesus Himself declared all foods clean (Mark 7:19). On the contrary, nowhere does Jesus or the New Testament scriptures declare homosexuality as a healthy option.

Here's some New Testament verses to know—and when you read these, if homosexuality is not the issue you deal with, pay attention to the other sins that prevent us from being free in Christ.

♡ *Even their women exchanged natural sexual relations for unnatural ones. In the same way the men also abandoned natural relations with women and were inflamed with lust for one another. Men committed shameful acts with other men, and received in themselves the due penalty for their error. (Romans 1:26–27 NIV)*

♡ *The law is made not for the righteous but for lawbreakers and rebels, the ungodly and sinful, the unholy and irreligious, for those who kill their fathers or mothers, for murderers, for the sexually immoral, for those practicing homosexuality, for slave traders and liars and perjurers—and for whatever else is contrary to the sound doctrine that conforms to the gospel. (1 Timothy 1:9–11 NIV)*

All the writers of the Bible were in agreement on this issue. Therefore it is not a cultural issue of the day; it is a universal standard in scripture.[7]

What Choices Do We Have?

We can never stop loving. We can accept but not approve. We can thank people for telling us their truths. We can help them in their struggles. And we can offer options.

Options to come to church. Options to serve in church. Options to come to Bible study and support groups and concerts and picnics and feed-the-poor campaigns. We have lots of options in the church. Trouble with finances? Trouble with parenting? Trouble with porn? Grieving a loss? Getting divorced? Getting married? Fighting addictions? Depression? Post-abortive? Transsexual? Bisexual? Gay? Lesbian?

How about those last four, folks? How about it!

You cannot just tell a gay person to become straight; being gay has to do with a lot more than sexual orientation—it has to do with community and beliefs and a sense of belonging. Being gay can be an identity.

One of the deepest desires I have is to teach people their identity in Christ. We are the beloved, the chosen, the redeemed; we are daughters, temples, lights, ambassadors. It is no different with the LGBT community—their identity in Christ must become primary. As it becomes primary, it can override their sexual identity. From there, people can find the route that is best for them.

One of those routes may be celibacy—deciding to stay single and have no sex with anyone—and this is something

7. Ibid., 91.

to be taken very seriously for people considering this option; there is no easy decision here.

Biblically, celibacy is celebrated. As marriage is celebrated, celibacy is celebrated. Paul was celibate—Jesus, too. Paul called it a gift that he wished everyone had.[8] He considered it a freedom.

God gives different prescriptions to each of us. Each of us must decide how to live as God designed us to live, as outlined by scripture, and be at peace with Him.

This is the struggle common to all—and all is possible through Christ who gives us strength. All.[9]

No Fear

P.S.: There is no fear in love, for perfect love drives out fear.[10] It's almost weird for me now not to feel fearful. But love has driven it out, and it feels fantastic to be free. Let's find ways to pursue people in the LGBT community and to love them in uncommon ways.

---

8. 1 Corinthians 7:7
9. For a more complete teaching on the tension between grace and truth for the LGBT community, see Caleb's book *Messy Grace*. He also has recommended reading in the back—which you can find on urmore.org/facts.php.
10. 1 John 4:18

A Few Grace Points:

💛 Being unloving to gay people is a sin. It's the opposite of being Christlike.

💛 As Christians, we should pursue those who struggle with sexual temptation so we can share God's love with them.

💛 All have sinned and fall short of the glory of God; we are all God's children, and He wants all His children to come home. This should be our primary focus.

💛 Kindness, not condemnation, leads people to repentance.

💛 Eternal life with Christ is available for all who believe and seek to live according to His Word.

💛 None of us is perfect at this, but God gives us the power to walk in the fullness of Christ, no matter what our struggle is.

MYTH 15:

Prostitutes, Strippers, and Porn Stars Are Dirty.

(And good girls don't become them.)

—

TRUTH 15:

There Are Hookers for Jesus.

(And they might just humble you. . .)

LIFE VERSE:

"Her sins, which are many, are forgiven—for she loved much. But he who is forgiven little, loves little." And [Jesus] said to her, "Your sins are forgiven."

LUKE 7:47–48 ESV

Violence Heard in Heaven

I can't look at porn. I just can't. The moment I see a woman selling her body on the screen, my heart breaks for her. Maybe I'm just sensitive that way; maybe I imagine too much of the heartache they bear. My mind races: *What happened to them when they were little girls? Where was her daddy? Was he absent or too busy or abusive or mean? Does her mama know, or was her body the first bed violated?*

What must it look like when the cameras are off! How sore they must be, how demeaned, how tired, how used, how sorry. How many abortions, diseases, beatings, break-ups, men? And for how much money? As if sex and money and men can fill the human heart with what we need to survive.

It is violence.

I've given you a word picture at the start of each chapter—the mud, the wolves, the letters in sand. The picture here is of a house. Robbers break in and steal, leaving things in disarray. Because the windows are left open and the doors crashed in, more looters come, and the girl inside is cuffed and hiding, naked and bare. Then a force so abrupt and so powerful comes whipping through that house that it appears never to have been in order in the first place. This is a wicked violence: a great, destructive force, damaging all the property. The parts and pieces fall jagged on top of the girl; she shakes and the walls shudder. Then, a gale comes clashing through, jarring everything unsteady, whipping the pictures and dreams off the walls in a furious explosion. The walls cave. Everything crashes. The girl is bloody and broken, demolished, destroyed.

Sexual sin is violence to the soul, a murderer of the heart, ravaging body and mind.

Satan is the destroyer. He tries to steal anything that

God means for good and turn it for evil; but our God turns evil into good, and our God is on high (and at His name the demons shudder).

Porn is not just a little problem; it's an epidemic, and we are to run screaming from the burning building. Women with their bodies up for sale *destroy* lives. Demolish relationships. Rip whole families apart, both for the woman on the screen and the woman lonely in bed next to the addicted man. The woman on the screen is being stolen from, and she is stealing from; and the woman in the bed, married and miserable, is shackled, too.

A friend of mine named Nikki, whose husband violated their marriage with pornography and adultery nineteen of the twenty-three years they were married, writes, "I filed for divorce a month ago. I lost myself in the hurt and the pain. I'm in a place now trying to figure out who I am and getting to know myself all over again. It really is a form of abuse. He got very aggressive in the bedroom, and it was so uncomfortable to the point that I could feel the spiritual battle waging. War raging. I didn't want to be intimate anymore because it ruined love."

She is now busy trying to provide for her three boys and find a new normal after the divorce. "On a positive note, my job is going well and the boys are okay, and God has a plan and healing will come and I will rise above the ashes."

Like many women in a desperate search to feel beautiful, for years Nikki suffered from anorexia. The self-image of women is being violated, and there is a God who wants more for His daughters. Violence is heard in His land, and the violence is *in us.* God is sickened, and He cries for His children—and He heals.

Soul Violence

Hearts break and hearts ache, and we call it commonplace.

Kids apparently see porn by the time they are eleven these days, with their phones tucked in back pockets. Addictions to porn begin in the teens. The result is catastrophic. The real flesh and blood of his one-day wife, her real breasts, and the touch of her skin, is somehow not enough. If a boy has a porn problem before marriage, marriage will not magically fix it. He must be real and open about it and seek continual help, counseling, and accountability to really break free for the long haul.[1]

In marriage the union between man and wife is demolished by unfaithfulness. It can be recovered from, but it's a long and hard road none of us wants to walk. Jesus called "looking at a woman lustfully" adultery[2]—so porn is adultery in His eyes. The marriage bed is to be kept pure and honored by all, period.

It's so terribly sad to think that anything on a screen or in a hotel bedroom or on a stage could fill anyone's soul hunger. The only thing it fills us with is pain, regret, and broken pieces to pick up so we can "try to find out who we are again," as Nikki puts it.

We long to be filled, all of us. But we choose idols: idols of money, power, sex, greed, lust for control, material things, addictions. And there is not a woman in the world who wants to be considered fare. She may be up on the screen, and there is a lineup of reasons for how she got there. But she's not fare to God; she's a princess.

And He wants more for her.

Soul violence: porn, prostitutes, strippers, and whores.

1. A great resource in this area is Ted Roberts's book, *Pure Desire* (Minneapolis, MN: Bethany House, 1999).
2. Matthew 5:28

Violence is heard in our land, and it is loud in Jesus' ears. He hears their cries in the throes of heaven.

He beckons them home.

Annie's Story

Annie was a good girl. Her mother was kind and gentle, but her daddy was harsh and mean and sometimes hit her mom. Annie longed for his love but was terrified by his anger. As a child, she was taught to sing, "Yes, Jesus loves me, the Bible tells me so," in church every Sunday with Mama by her side. At nine, Annie was sexually abused by an older friend during their sleepovers. Annie wanted the approval of this older girl, so she hid the shame and guilt and told no one. She had her first kiss at nine and at the same time began attending a Christian elementary school where she learned to sing, "I've got the joy-joy-joy down in my heart." Annie had brothers and sisters who deeply loved her and a teacher who taught the kindness and unconditional love of Jesus.

But her family moved away in the sixth grade, and Annie looked everywhere for acceptance. Bullied and rejected by girls, in high school she sought solace in the arms of a handsome boy. Sure that she had found her prince in this striking football player, Annie told him at first that she wasn't ready for sex, but he put the pressure on. Then one night she got drunk at a party and a guy in his twenties led her to an upstairs room, and in the shadows of the night she clawed and fought as he ripped off her clothes and attempted to rape her.

She got away but then gave herself to her "prince," who shortly afterward revealed he was sleeping with three other girls and had no feelings for her. She graduated from high school, embittered and angry. The pain of betrayal and the continuing absence of fatherly affection snowballed into a hunger for revenge. Annie made it her mission to be "successful," to show everyone who the real boss was.[3]

Annie left home after high school, excited to pursue her dreams of becoming a career woman. Left on her own, she had to put herself through college. Determined, she worked days, nights, and weekends at three jobs in Minneapolis, Minnesota, to support herself and save for college at the same time. She loved the professional world, enjoyed dressing the part of a sharp-minded businesswoman, and continually lusted for more. As she became more successful, she wanted more money, more power, more freedom. She wanted the prince and the castle and held the story of Cinderella in her heart. Annie longed to be loved, valued, and taken care of, and she wanted a castle of her own—even if she had to buy it.

Working so hard for so little, she was becoming increasingly discontent with her life when her best friend, Kimmie, invited her on an all-expenses-paid trip to Hawaii with her boyfriend, a seemingly kind and generous man who appeared to love Kimmie.

Annie saw the way he spoiled Kimmie, lavishing her with dinners at expensive restaurants, fancy cars, elaborate hotel rooms, costly jewels, beautiful clothes, shoes, and purses. Annie wanted all of that, and Kimmie introduced her to the life of a "high-class escort."

Excited for their first night out to make some big bucks, Annie and Kimmie got all gussied up and blasted their favorite music, preparing for a hot night. Registered with an agency, they would earn five hundred dollars to one thousand dollars or more a night per appointment just to undress in front of the polite Japanese businessmen who

3. Annie Lobert, *Fallen* (Brentwood, TN: Worthy, 2015), 15.

came to Hawaii. In the beginning, there was no sex. Just fancy cars and clothes and money, money, money flowing like a fountain into their pockets! Annie figured out pretty quickly that by being seductive she could get practically anything she wanted.[4]

Kimmie's "knight in shining armor" brought them from Hawaii to Beverly Hills to Vegas, and Annie made more money than she knew what to do with "turning tricks"—or performing sexual favors. The night lights, the bars, the liquor, the cars, the clothes. . .she wanted it all, and began to get it all.

If you think of yourself as a "good" girl, you may have passed judgment on Annie. But if you read her page-turning book *Fallen,* as I did one long and languid morning, you will find out she was not motivated by a lust for sex. She was in a desperate lunge for love; she wanted money, and more and more money never was enough. Being a call girl and a stripper would be her secret way of making it in life. She wanted the reins; she wanted to take control of her future and destiny. She danced on stages while men threw wads of money at her feet, and the powerful monster of greed took over her heart.[5]

Then one day, in walked her own prince charming: sweet, smart, handsome, adoring Julian. She fell madly in love while continuing to work for the escort service for the next five years. "*Clients would call the agency and operators, or 'phone girls' would match them with the appropriate working girl, a barely eighteen busty blonde, a slim and tan brunette college girl, an Asian beauty, a racy redhead housewife, and so on. . .and their phone was ringing off the hook with requests for 'hot young blonde, barely eighteen.'*"[6]

---

4. Ibid., 26.
5. Ibid., 28, 29, 37, 39.
6. Ibid., 57.

One night she came home with eight hundred dollars from just one appointment, and Julian demanded her purse. *Who does he think he is?* She thought, *I would never pay a pimp! This is my money!*

She sassed him, and he grabbed her by the throat, slammed her against the cupboard, and she blacked out. Grabbing her by the hair, he dragged her outside, dirtying her fresh, new white suit, and pounded away at her, punching her in the face and kicking her in the ribs as the Las Vegas sky blurred above, the illusion of glamour twisting into a confused picture of rage.

Annie begged him to stop, but her cries fell on deaf ears. Kimmie screamed, but her boyfriend/pimp locked her in the bedroom so she couldn't help Annie.

Julian flipped Annie's body over and grabbed the back of her neck, dragging her deeper into the yard, and shoved her face in fresh dog poop. Pieces of her broken teeth filled her mouth. Broken ribs made it hard to breathe. She screamed; she cried.

Helpless, she was caught in the grips of an abuser, and it would be several years before she could escape.

Over the course of her life as a call girl, Annie was beaten by Julian multiple times. In another instance, she was raped by a man who held a gun to her head.

She had seven abortions and three miscarriages.

Every time Julian beat her, he charmed her with money and gifts and tears of remorse, convincing her he loved her and would change. And she loved him back. She stayed with him, tried to flee, then went back to her abuser again and again, as many women do.

A pimp gains control through brainwashing. He lavishes love and valuables upon a girl until she is emotionally engrossed in him, convinced he is her savior, and then uses that love as a weapon to make her his slave.[7] As soon as a girl starts believing she cannot live without him, the pimp has her right where he wants her. He makes her dependent on him physically, emotionally, mentally. If she tries to escape, he beats her into submission. So she is terrified to leave. She becomes a captive to his control, a prisoner of pain.

Strikingly Beautiful

Annie's self-esteem was long gone; pleasing Julian became her life. But whenever she planned escape, he assured her he would hunt her down and often told her he was going to bury her "six feet under in the desert."

And hunt her down he did. He took away her driver's license so she had no identification. She couldn't open up a bank account if she tried. He stole her identity, her worth. For five years, she was the object of his sickness. He had other slaves, too, and a deep-seated porn addiction, and he was in trouble with the law. And he had Annie's heart, body, and soul behind bars.

Mentally, she kept planning her escape, and Julian sensed it. Right before leaving on a trip, he took out his revolver and forced her into the garage, tied her up, and made her get in the trunk of his car. Her eyes saw a body bag and a shovel. Sure that he was finally going to make good on his threats to "bury her six feet under in the desert," she screamed, cried, and begged for him to stop, but he just slammed closed the trunk and turned on the car, leaving the garage door closed.

Sure that she would die of carbon monoxide poisoning, Annie's mind suddenly flooded with fond memories of eating

---

7. Ibid., 63.

treats while listening to Bible stories in Sunday school. From the trunk of the car, she began singing loudly, "Jesus loves me, this I know, for the Bible tells me so. Little ones to Him belong; they are weak but He is strong, Yes, Jesus loves me. Yes, Jesus loves me; yes, Jesus loves me, the Bible tells me so."

Appalled, he shut off the car, threw her back in the house, and left for his trip.

Annie got away, but he found her.

When he did, he beat her senseless in front of other pimps and prostitutes, "making an example of her" to show the other girls what would happen if they tried to run. While she crawled naked, bloody, and beaten on the floor, he whipped her with a fireplace poker, severing a muscle in her leg. He even shaved off her luscious long blonde hair and beat her late into the night, making another young girl sit next to Annie's blood-caked and torn-up body to contemplate what would happen to that girl if she ever tried to leave.

After many attempts, Annie finally broke free from Julian.

But a drug addiction ensued, a way to escape the pain, and finally she overdosed on cocaine. As the paramedics tried to resuscitate her, Annie cried out over and over for Jesus to save her.

And save her He did.

I hope neither you nor I will ever see a porn star, stripper, prostitute, or sex slave the same again. Annie Lobert is a survivor of over a decade of sex trafficking. She started out trying to put herself through college, and she ended up a slave.

The enemy tried to destroy her, but she will tell you to this day that Jesus saved her and is bringing beauty from the brokenness.

Annie was delivered from drug addiction the day of her overdose, but she wanted to *see* Jesus, to *know* Him, to *yada*.

One night He answered her prayer. In a dream she was sitting at a bus stop in New York City, and a man with long brown hair dressed in a flowing robe started walking toward her. He was magnetic; she couldn't keep her eyes off Him, and she knew it was Jesus.

Annie describes him as "strikingly beautiful, with strong facial features, chiseled in defining angles," and his eyes were "radiant with light."

He reached out toward her and told her how special she was to Him, how He had seen every horrible thing she had been through, how none of it was right, and He assured her that He was there for her, that she was never alone, and that He had loved her since the beginning of time.

He promised her that the tragedies she had endured would become a bridge to heal others and that He would be her source of life now.

Jesus also told her that He had an incredible purpose for her that only she could fulfill—to go down to the Las Vegas Strip and tell the women who are enslaved how much He loves them, how He can heal their broken hearts, and all that He had done for her.[8]

Today Annie runs a ministry in Vegas called Hookers for Jesus. She has founded the Destiny House, named after a child she miscarried who she believed never had a chance to fill her life's purpose. The Destiny House offers women in the sex industry the chance for a new life. It is a free twelve-month program to help women escape from and reestablish their lives outside the sex industry. Their program treats the whole person with emotional, mental, spiritual, relational, and physical healing. Annie believes that each woman who

8. Ibid., 167–269.

comes to the Destiny House will have a brand-new chance to fulfill her God-given destiny. She calls them overcomers of their pasts who will change the world for the good.[9]

The Woman Who Was a Sinner

When the Pharisees, or religious leaders, had a fancy-schmancy dinner at their house, Jesus was kicking it at the table when a woman "who had lived a sinful life" approached Him at His feet, crying and wetting His feet with her tears.

People claimed He shouldn't let her touch Him.

But Jesus knew her already. He knew all the ways she had been used and abused, all the ways she had been hurt. He knew her story and her worth.

And He who "had done no violence" knew the overwhelming force that had crumbled her to the ground in such agony. He knew about every robber, every jagged blow, every broken piece of glass in her shattered heart. He knew the whipping in the soul of a prostitute.

She fell at His feet in surrender. Of all people, she knew how badly she needed Him.

He loved her so much for that. He stood up right in front of all those fancy-schmancy people and said so—how much she loved, and how much He loved her, too, and forgave her.

Prostitutes, sinners, and saints: we are all precious in His eyes.

Now, if we could just love others the way He loves us. . . stand up, defend, and extend our hands to those who have had a violence in the soul, from one mercy-lined mess to another.

---

9. See www.hookersforjesus.net to find out how you can support their work.

MYTH 16:

Sexual Encounters That Hurt Are Okay.

(Risky is fun, but I won't get raped.)

~

TRUTH 16:

Sex Is Best When It's Safe and Secure.

(It's up to you to protect what is precious.)

LIFE VERSE:

*His left hand is under my head,
and his right hand embraces me.*

SONG OF SOLOMON 2:6 NKJV

No Shades of Grey

When the film *Fifty Shades of Grey* came out, a wave of controversy exploded. People got caught up in what is "right and wrong," tangled in the shadows of sex like a sticky spiderweb. Instead of paying close attention to what is black-and-white and red-letter, people talked about "what is okay for you" and "okay for me."

In black-and-white and red-letter, we know that Jesus does "no wrong," and is "humble and gentle at heart"; that "he came not to be served but to serve."[1] One must be able to see Satan's ploy when in the movie the man is named "Christian," yet *he beats the object of his lust for sexual pleasure and calls it love.*

The movie is based on the typical vampire myth: the charming, handsome, rich guy gains control of a girl who wants love and affection, and all along he is sucking the lifeblood right out of her through manipulation and control. And she keeps coming back for more lashings.

After Adam and Eve disobeyed God, violence filled the earth.[2] And people have been trying to explain away the shades of grey ever since. "I killed him *because. . .*" "I lied *because. . .*" "I stole *because. . .*" "I hit her *because. . .*" Then, one day, it was I "killed the author of life because. . ." Jesus Himself was whipped, mocked, beaten, and humiliated to His death—but He never dreamed of humiliating or beating us. If you have ever experienced humiliation, I just want to remind you: He rose from it, and so can you.

There are a lot of sick things in this world. One of them is beating or harming another human being for sexual pleasure.

---

1. Isaiah 53:9; Matthew 11:29; Matthew 20:28
2. Genesis 6:11

Annie knows what rape does to a soul, the torment.

In all the years I've been with the Cowboy, our bed sheets have only been graced by gentleness and peace. There has never been fear or shame or pain.

I have a very passionate relationship with my husband. But sex has never been scary or painful, and neither has he ever attempted to harm me. I am safe and secure in his arms.

And you deserve nothing less. There are no shades of grey here. It is black-and-white, red.

No matter what twisted way Hollywood tries to lie to us, picturing abuse in movies as plausibly attractive and exciting, we walk in truth: God speaks in gentle and adoring tones to His beloved. He would never whip us, for it is contrary to His nature. He would never hit us! Nor would he pressure us into doing something that made us feel vulnerable or afraid. Jesus did no violence, nor did He ever speak a lie.

Check out the tone of the Bible's book on love, the Song of Songs. See how God paints sex in soft tones, sunshine like gold next to a trickling stream. Here He pictures a man and his bride in the same way that Christ loves the church:

> *He brought me to the banquet hall, and he looked on me with love. . . . My love calls to me: Arise, my darling, Come away, my beautiful one. . . . Let me see your face, let me hear your voice; for your voice is sweet and your face is lovely. . . . His eyes are like doves beside streams of water, washed in milk and set like jewels. . . Come, my love, let's go to the field; let's spend the night among the henna blossoms. . . .There I will give you my love. . . His left hand is under my head, and his right arm embraces me. (Song of Songs*

2:4, 10, 14; 5:12; 7:11–12, 8:3; 2–6 HCSB)

These adoring words show the complete safety we should have in our lover's arms.

How I want to cup your face in my hands right now and tell you how sacred sex is! How safe relationships should be! You should never fear that your boyfriend or husband will physically harm you. If you do, get out of the relationship!

You are too holy to be harmed. Too precious to be used. Too priceless for a price tag. Too valuable to be exposed, controlled, or dominated. All of this grieves our Father in heaven who loves us.

Don't Want to but Have To. . .

I don't want to have to define these terms for you, but I'm going to. Knowledge is understanding, a rare treasure to she who embraces it. So more knowledge and understanding is better than less.

Let's define a few tough terms here, and you decide for yourself if they are helpful or harmful. The Bible says "everything is permissible" for us, but not everything is beneficial: *"'Everything is permissible for me,' but I will not be brought under the control of anything"* (1 Corinthians 6:12 HCSB).

BDSM is a term that stands for *bondage, dominance, sadism, and masochism*. These are sexual practices that we don't find in the romantic pursuit of the Song of Songs, and they are as far removed from God's picture of love for you as the east is from the west. But they do exist in the world, and I want you to know what they are.

♡ Bondage: Tying, binding, or restraining someone for

sexual or psychological pleasure. This could involve handcuffs, tape, ropes, or other restraints.

♡ Dominance: The action of taking on a forcefully authoritative role over another, which may include sexual slavery, humiliation, or whipping.

♡ Sadism: Sexual enjoyment that someone gets from being violent or cruel or from hurting or punishing someone. A sadist is a person who uses bondage and dominance to inflict pain or humiliation on another.

♡ Masochism: Sexual enjoyment from being abused, hurt, or punished. A masochist is a person who enjoys receiving pain from another.

Test It!

The Bible teaches us to "test everything; hold fast what is good. Abstain from every form of evil" (1 Thessalonians 5:21–22 ESV). So let's test BDSM.

God compares the relationship between a man and his wife to Christ and the church: "Wives, submit to your own husbands as to the Lord, for the husband is the head of the wife as Christ is the head of the church. He is the Savior of the body" (Ephesians 5:22–23 HCSB).

So we are to honor our husbands as the head of our homes, and as we do that, our husbands in turn take the role of the Savior of the body. Not the harmer. Not the violator. The Savior.

The passage continues: "Husbands are to love their wives as their own bodies. . . . For no one ever hates his own flesh, but provides and cares for it, just as Christ does for the church, since we are members of His body" (Ephesians 5:28–30 HCSB).

Ask yourself, and answer for yourself, in the quiet of your heart: *Would Jesus ever mock or insult me? Tie me up and rape me? Hit me? Beat me? Would He ever try to convince me to agree to such a thing?*

There is a passage from Isaiah that sums it up: "Woe to those who call evil good and good evil, who substitute darkness for light and light for darkness, who substitute bitter for sweet and sweet for bitter" (Isaiah 5:20 HCSB).

Sex is sweet. God never intended it to be bitter. Sex is good. But like anything, it can be used for evil. Love is patient, kind, gentle, and faithful—and real love never fails. Some people believe that if they expose themselves to pornography, BDSM, or multiple partners, they will experience a more fulfilling and exciting sex life. This couldn't be further from the truth. Real sexual fulfillment comes from sex that is safe and sweet. The best sexual enjoyment comes not from lust, but from love. It comes from not only joining your body with the one you love, but also by joining your soul in deep abiding friendship and respect. Fulfilling sex requires respect and security to taste as sweet as God desires it to be.

Only allow yourself to experience sex that is safe and free from harm. Never allow yourself to be belittled, abused, shamed, or hit by anyone. Don't let anyone steal your worth that way.

Finally, know the difference between lust and love. Love is gradual. Love gives. Love is controlled. Love lasts. Put to memory the following chart so you will know the difference and live by it.[3]

3. June Hunt, *Counseling through Your Bible Handbook* (Harvest House, 2008), 376–377.

Lust Is:

temporary
sudden
selfish
untrustworthy
impatient
uncontrolled desire
emotionally shallow
based on fantasy
full of emotion
driven by one's passion
focused on external looks
set on getting happiness
eager to get

Love Is:

enduring
gradual
unselfish
trustworthy
patient
controlled desire
emotionally deep
based on reality
full of devotion
chosen by one's will
focused on internal character
set on giving happiness
eager to give

Passionately pursue love. It will guide your steps, heal your heart, and give you hope to live in a way that honors both you and your heavenly Father.

Who Gets the Key?

So if your body is God's house, who gets the key? Determining in advance who has the key to your heart—and your body—can go a long way toward determining your actions sexually. When you give God the key, reserving your body in godliness, and self-control and for your future husband, you will naturally put guards in place to protect what is valuable: *you*.

But what happens when a woman/girl gives her keys away and then gets stolen from? She gives a guy the key to her body—she climbs into his bed late at night, invites him to her apartment alone, or is parked in a secluded place making out with him. She thinks she can trust him, but he's actually a wolf in sheep's clothing. When the level of sexual activity makes her uncomfortable or violates her boundaries, she says, *"No. Stop."*

She clearly communicates she does not want to continue.

But due to his hunger for power or misbelief that he is not responsible for his own actions, he takes more than she wants him to; he forces himself on her. He either sexually assaults or rapes her. Is it her fault? After all, she did open the door and let him in.

No.

No one invites rape. In every single case, there is no excuse for sexual assault. The rapist, or robber as we are calling him, is at fault every time. He can't cry out and say, "Well, she gave me the key! So I thought I had every right to take everything in the house!" when in truth she *trusted* him with what was precious, and he stole from her. He violated the sanctity of her heart, body, and soul, and that is his responsibility.

On the other hand, what happens when someone breaks right through the door and steals what is precious to you: your body? In this case, the girl gets caught totally unaware— tricked, attacked, assaulted, her face shoved into the mud— and the boy/man forces himself on her; he rapes her.

In both cases, the girl gets robbed, *and the robber is the only one to blame.*

But in the first case, it honestly could have been pre- vented. The girl/woman chose to invite the man up to her apartment or climbed in his bed or went to a secluded place, possibly late at night or under the influence of alcohol; she chose to get naked or share her body with him. So she invited the robber into the house, not realizing he was a robber. But in the final analysis, *as soon as she said* no, *he should have stopped.* Any time sexual activity turns into selfish taking, it is wrong.

Sex should never involve force.

Sexual contact should always be consensual—meaning both people enthusiastically agree.

Rape is a decision made by the rapist. He is the one who decided that his desires were more important than her value.

Did you know?[4]

♥ 4 out of 5 assaults are committed by someone known to the victim.

♥ 47% of rapists are a friend or acquaintance.

♥ 80% of sexual assault victims are under the age of 30.

♥ Every 107 seconds, another American is sexually assaulted.

♥ 68% of sexual assaults are not reported to police.

♥ 1 in 6 American women will be sexually assaulted in her lifetime.

What Is Consensual Sex?

In sexual assault cases, the judge wants to know one thing: was it consensual? In other words, did both people agree

4. Statistics taken from Rape, Abuse and Incest National Network, rainn.org.

to the sexual activity, or was one person not in agreement?

Consent is a mutually agreed upon decision to engage in sexual activity. Both people express a desire to kiss, touch, or have sex. Consent is best when it is clearly communicated prior to sexual engagement, and communication about what is okay should happen every time.

A few things to know about consent:[5]

♡ Giving consent for one activity one time does not mean giving consent for increased or recurring sexual contact. For example, agreeing to kiss someone once does not give that person permission to kiss you again. Agreeing to kiss someone also doesn't give that person permission to touch your privates or remove your clothes. Likewise, having sex with someone in the past doesn't give that person permission to have sex with you again in the future.

♡ You can change your mind at any time. You can withdraw consent at any point you feel uncomfortable. It's important to clearly communicate to the other person that you are no longer comfortable with this activity and wish to stop.

♡ Healthy consent can look like this:

• Communicating when you change the type or degree of sexual activity with phrases like "Is this okay?" and respecting and stopping if the other person says no

• Clearly saying yes or no to certain activities

♡ Healthy consent *does not* look like this:

• Refusing to acknowledge *no*

• Assuming that wearing certain clothes, flirting, or kissing is an invitation for anything more

5. https://rainn.org/get-information/sexual-assault-prevention/what-is-consent

- Someone being under the legal age of consent, as defined by the state

- Someone being incapacitated because of drugs or alcohol

- Pressuring someone into sexual activity by using fear or intimidation

- Assuming you have permission to engage in a sexual act because you've done so in the past

You have the right to protect your body and enforce your boundaries. You don't have to give any more affection than what you want to, and you have the right to say no. Just remember that consent is an "enthusiastic yes" on the part of both people, and anything outside of that violates the holiness of sex.

Reducing Your Risk of Rape

If someone is pressuring you, there are some things you can do to get out of the situation:[6]

- ♡ Remember it's not your fault. If you are in an uncomfortable situation and the other person wants something you don't want, it's not your fault.

- ♡ Trust your gut. It doesn't matter why you don't want to do something; not being interested is reason enough. You don't need to explain yourself. Only do what feels right to you and what you are comfortable with.

- ♡ Have a code word. Develop a code with friends or family that means "I'm uncomfortable" or "I need

---

6. Information compiled from rainn.org, "How to Respond if Someone Is Pressuring You," "Staying Safe on Campus," and "Alcohol Safety."

help." It could be a number you can text, like 311, or a phrase you say out loud. This way the person you are alerting can help you right away.

♡ Make an excuse to exit. If you are concerned you might anger or upset this person, you can lie or make an excuse to exit. You are never obligated to remain in a situation that makes you feel uncomfortable. Make an excuse why you need to leave, like you have to be somewhere at a certain time or you need to take care of a friend or family member. Even excusing yourself to the bathroom can create an opportunity to get away. Even if it seems embarrassing at the time, it's okay for you to say whatever you need to say to stay safe.

♡ Think of an escape route. If you had to leave quickly, how would you do it? Locate the windows, doors, and any other means of exiting the situation. Are there people around you who could help you? How would you get their attention? Where can you go when you leave?

♡ On college campuses, don't just assume you're in a safe environment. There are a few key things you can do to prevent sexual assault and take care of your most important asset: you.

♡ Know your resources. Who will you contact if you or a friend needs help? Where will you go? Know where the campus police station is and the campus health center. Program the campus security number into your cell for easy access.

♡ Stay alert. Be aware of your surroundings when moving around campus or in the surrounding neighborhood, especially at night. You can always ask a friend to go with you or request a campus security escort. If you are alone, don't use headphones or earbuds in your ears so you can stay alert to your surroundings.

♡ Don't post your location. Many social media sites track and post your location. You can disable this function so others don't know your location all the time.

♡ Make others earn your trust. A college environment can create a false sense of security. People may feel like fast friends, but give them time to earn your trust.

♡ Make a Plan B. Think about back-up plans for sticky situations. If your phone dies, have a few phone numbers memorized to get help. Carry emergency cash in case you can't use a credit card. Memorize the address to your dorm. If you drive, keep a spare key hidden. Carry jumper cables, and make sure you have enough gas to get home at all times.

In Social Situations. . .

♡ Choose not to drink alcohol. Alcohol weakens your body's natural defense mechanisms as well as your ability to make good decisions. Just because others are drinking doesn't mean you have to. You can choose not to drink and keep your decision-making rock solid.

♡ Know your limits. If you choose to drink, decide in advance how much you will drink, and keep track of how many drinks you've had. Drink water after you've reached your limit. If you feel extremely tired or drunk, ask a friend for help and find a way to get home safely as soon as possible.

♡ Protect your drink. Don't leave your food or drink unattended, and watch out for your friends' drinks. If you go to the bathroom or step outside, take the drink with you or toss it out. Drink from unopened containers or drinks you watched being made and poured.

♡ Make a plan. Make a pact with a friend that says, "If we go out together, we come home together," and stick to it!

♡ Be a good friend. Trust your instincts. If something

doesn't seem right with a friend, it probably isn't. Stepping in can save another girl's life. According to the Rape, Abuse, and Incest National Network (RAINN), a good friend knows how to C.A.R.E:

- Create a distraction. Find a way to interrupt the situation that looks risky for your friend. Cut off the conversation with a diversion like "Let's get pizza. I'm starving," or "This party is lame. Let's go." You can also spark a conversation with the people you are concerned about by offering them to play a game or eat something.

- Ask directly. Ask questions like "Who did you come here with?" or "Would you like me to stay with you?"

- Refer to an authority. Talk to a security guard or employee about your concerns. They will usually be willing to step in. Don't hesitate to call 911.

- Enlist others. Ask someone to come with you to approach the person at risk, or ask someone to intervene in your place.

In the case that someone is attempting to violate you, try to get away if at all possible. First try a diversion to draw their attention to something else. Scream and yell for help. Fight, claw, and kick. Try to cut off their air supply or gouge out their eyes. Go into focused madwoman mode—your focus is survival. One tip is if they are trying to choke you, pull up on their thumbs—because that is the weakest part of their body. Bottom line: do everything you possibly can to survive.

If you are assaulted, please remember it is not your fault—something happened to you that you did not want to have happen, and you can recover. You matter, and you deserve to be protected. Stand up for yourself and report it. Immediately. Don't shower. Don't change clothes or underwear. Get to a safe place and call the police or the National Sexual Assault Hotline at 800.656.HOPE (4673).

People need to be held accountable for sexual crimes against the innocent. Reporting sexual assault may prevent that person from hurting more victims.

Sexual assault can cause tremendous physical, mental, and emotional anguish. Never judge a woman who has been assaulted. Instead, invite her into the possibility of healing through Christ. If you have been sexually abused or assaulted, get to a counselor as soon as you can. You are worth doing the hard work of healing your heart. Find a way to bring beauty from the ashes.

And know this: Jesus receives you with grace. Whatever the circumstances, you are precious to Him. Your body is precious; your sexuality, too.

MYTH 17:

Sex Is a Normal Part of Dating.
(Some TV shows, magazines, and adults say so—
aren't they telling the truth?)

~

TRUTH 17:

Sex Is a Normal Part of Marriage.
(Learn to control yourself now;
it's good practice for later!)

LIFE VERSE:
Young women. . . I charge you. . .
do not stir up or awaken love
until the appropriate time.
SONG OF SONGS 2:7 HCSB

What We're Up Against

Sex within marriage is kind of like playing in your own backyard: you are on your own property! You are safe, and you can run inside if you see a storm coming. Sex outside of marriage is more like sneaking into the neighbor's house. You are not on your own property, you could get caught any second, and your heart is beating a mile a minute. It's risky. There is *no* safe place, unless you go *home*.

Here's what we're up against: in movies, on TV, in popular music, on college campuses, and even in some high schools, sexual activity is painted as a normal part of dating. Many of the spokespeople for these outlets are working overtime to make sexual sin look as normal as going to the store.

When I open a fashion magazine, I see article after article about how to please yourself, your boyfriend, or your same-sex lover, with a major downplay on marriage as the ideal format for these very intimate and personal experiences. Why would we want to have our most private, bare-naked sexual exchanges with a "boyfriend" who could leave us? Who may not be ready to raise our child? Who maybe we don't even want to marry? When we are in our teens and early twenties, we often don't realize how *passing* most dating relationships are. So we give a boyfriend what is precious in hopes of making love last—and most times it doesn't.

Back in the day, when our moms and grandmas were growing up, people didn't even show *married* sex on TV. Some of the most popular shows of the 1950s didn't show husbands and wives even sleeping in the same bed—they slept in *separate* beds! And the women climbed into the covers wearing full-length, long-sleeved nightgowns, curlers in their hair, and blinders over their eyes—not so they could arouse their husbands—so that they could sleep! Today it's the opposite. Women on TV are seen in sensual poses that at one time were for their *husbands' eyes only.* Windows at the mall are wallpapered with very young women wearing (not-your-grandmother's) underwear. We see sexual relationships on TV between two men, two women, or with more than one person. Whether or not these characters are in lifelong relationships is usually not even considered. As portrayed by media, sex, the body, and marriage are not sacred at all.

The result? We have a world full of women and girls churning with angst because they believed the myths. They believed they could give their bodies away without getting their hearts hurt. But the big screen can be a big fat liar. Movies, music videos, and magazines don't show how much regret sex outside of marriage can cause. And this is the other thing the movies don't show: the best, be-still-your-soul, filled-with-security sex you can ever have is the married kind. There is no shame, regret, or remorse in married sex that is safe, loving—and feels great.

And that's what we all want.

Famous Love

Real sensuality is not painted on the covers of monthly magazines. The most sensual love poem ever written is God-breathed, in the center of the bestselling book of all time, your Bible.

Set in a vineyard, the Song of Songs is theorized to suggest the mysterious connection between Christ and His bride, the church. And if that is so, *He sure does love His bride!* He pictures us as the essence of attraction, the image of true, genuine beauty. To be one with us is His greatest desire.

Song of Songs is also the ooh-la-la sex book of the

Bible, suggesting romance and the pursuit of love as the ultimate experience of a man and woman. In this symbolic, metaphorical poem, attraction and desire kiss love and commitment, and sex bears fruit to soul-knowing.

In its most literal sense, the Songs of Songs is about the romance between a real man and woman, Solomon and his bride, the Shulamite woman. Its colorful poetry paints a picture of the allure of sex as a tender and passionate embrace. In the Song of Songs, we see true love that pursues, waits for the right time, and ripens with age.

The poem begins with the woman's voice: "Oh, that he would kiss me with the kisses of his mouth! For your love is more delightful than wine. The fragrance of your perfume is intoxicating. . . . Take me with you—let us hurry. Oh, that the king would bring me to his chambers" (Song of Songs 1:2–4 HCSB).

This is pretty bold of the little lady, don't you think? It's not exactly the traditional "boy pursues girl" from the get-go! The woman makes herself vulnerable and lays her cards right on the table. "*Kiss me! Take me with you!*" she says to him.

This is the yearning Christ desires from us. "Pursue Me!" the Lord tells us. "Abide in My love, and I will abide in you. Seek Me with all your heart, and I will be found by you."

But in the very next line of the poem, the woman shrinks back and her insecurities rush forward. In those cards she laid right on the table, her heart fears comparison. She is afraid she is not as beautiful as the other women, and she openly says so. "Do not stare at me because I am dark, for the sun has gazed on me" (Song of Songs 1:6 HCSB). Hers was not the day of spray tans; in fact, her tanned skin revealed she was from the lower working class, not like the king in his royalty.

But from the first moment the king opens his mouth, he assures her of her beauty; he fills the desire of every woman's heart, to know that he is not comparing her to others—but sees her unique beauty and calls it forth. He also vows to create expensive jewelry for her to wear.

His declaration of her beauty and value immediately puts her at ease, and she responds by describing her love like a sachet of myrrh, an incensed oil, tucked between her breasts, a cluster of blossoms by a wellspring of water.

He says to her *again:* "How beautiful you are, my darling. How very beautiful! Your eyes are doves" (Song of Songs 1:15 HCSB).

She responds by saying how handsome he is, by describing their bed as a lush garden. She compares herself to a rose, and her groom to an apricot tree where she loves to sit beneath his shade, enjoying his fruit sweet to the taste.

They are longing for each other, yearning to be together. Her groom ushers her to come away with him, takes her to the banquet hall, and looks upon her with love. Then he embraces her—and she *stops*! Right there, right at the moment of embrace, when his left hand is under her head and his right hand holds her, she puts her hand up! She turns her attention from her groom to the young women watching.

I Charge You. . .

"I charge you," she says, "by the gazelles and the wild does of the field: do not stir up or awaken love until the appropriate time" (Song of Songs 2:7 HCSB).

Why would she do this? She is thirsting to be with her man. They are dripping with desire, and he is calling her to come away.

You would think he is everything to her. But he is not *all*!

The purity of his pursuit turns her attention to the younger women, for her to say—Wait!

Wait! Don't mess this up for yourself! I want this for you too! I want you to be pursued; to be longed for; to be desired; to be told you are beautiful. But I don't want you to arouse yourself before the right time. I don't want you to arouse your groom before it's right. Let him pursue you, but show restraint. Do not arouse or awaken love before the appropriate time. He should adorn you with jewelry and feed you fine food, and you should delight in his presence, and he should take you to the banquet hall to make it all official in front of everyone. That is the romance. That is the pursuit.

And you are worth the pursuit. Worth waiting for. (And if he doesn't see that, tell him your sachet of myrrh and your well of flowing water are for your groom, and get out of there!)

As she waits for her love, longing for his presence, she says it again: "Young women of Jerusalem, I charge you, by the gazelles and the wild does of the field; do not stir up or awaken love until the appropriate time" (Song of Songs 3:5 HCSB).

Yearning for the moment she will be with her love, the woman waits until the wedding day comes, and the groom's companions gather around; her friends are also there. The king wears a crown his mother placed on him for "the day of his wedding—the day of his heart's rejoicing" (Song of Songs 3:11 HCSB). He praises his bride's beauty from head to toe, complimenting everything about her, and saying her eyes behind her veil are doves (Song of Songs 4:1 HCSB).

Over and over again, he calls her his bride, saying she has captured his heart with one glance of her eyes, one jewel of her necklace. He calls her to come away with him, for her love is better than wine and the fragrance of her perfume than any spice. He says her lips drip sweetness like the honeycomb; honey and milk are under her tongue.

He calls his bride "a locked garden and a sealed spring," showing value for her virginity, sealed and protected for him only (Song of Songs 4:12 HCSB).

Then the moment comes.

She invites him in: "Blow on my garden, and spread the fragrance of its spices. Let my love come to his garden and eat its choicest fruits" (Song of Songs 4:16 HCSB).

She calls her sexuality *her* garden; then in the next line, she calls it *his* garden.

He receives the gift of her body as his own.

"I have come to my garden—my sister, my bride," referring now to her as his own (Song of Songs 5:1 HCSB). "Sister" is also an affectionate term for "spouse."

"I eat my honeycomb with my honey," he says. "I drink my wine with my milk" (5:1 HCSB).

"Eat, friends!" the Word says, "Be intoxicated with love!" (Song of Songs 5:1–2 HCSB).

And the marriage is sealed.

In other passages, he describes her breasts like two fawns, twins of a gazelle, which feed among the lilies; and as clusters of grapes—he says he is going to climb the palm tree and take hold of its fruit. The woman describes taking off her clothing, and her love thrusting his hand through the opening while her fingers drip with myrrh on the handles of the bolt. She also visits the "walnut grove to see the blossoms of the valley" which literally means "garden of nuts," and describes his body as an "ivory panel covered with sapphires" (Song of Songs 6:11; 5:14).

When they are exploring the pomegranates (Song of

Songs 6:11; 7:12), they are enjoying the sexual exploration of one another's bodies, and all of this happens in the context of love and commitment—not dating. The garden blooms *after the wedding.*

The words are cryptic. Secret. Subtle.

It's not all spelled out like the songs of today.

It's not in-your-face, blatant, and obvious.

It's perfect poetry.

And it doesn't end. There is an understanding at the end of the poem that time has passed, and love has grown *stronger.*

> *Set me as a seal on your heart, as a seal on your arm, For love is as strong as death; ardent love is an unrelenting as Sheol. Love's flames are fiery flames— the fiercest of all. Mighty waters cannot extinguish love; rivers cannot sweep it away. (Song of Songs 8:6–7 HCSB)*

At the end of the poem the woman describes herself as secure in love, whereas at the beginning she was insecure: "In his eyes I have become like one who finds peace" (Song of Songs 8:10 HCSB).

This reminds me of one of my favorite scriptures: "Let the beloved of the LORD rest secure in him, for he shields him all day long and the one the LORD loves rests between his shoulders" (Deuteronomy 33:12 NIV).

In the end of the poem, love and desire are still in her heart, and peace is in her eyes.

The Pursuit of Knowing

Just as Christ says to His bride, you are beautiful, you are valuable, you are priceless. If you love someone, he should pursue you all the way to the wedding and beyond. And when you are united—in oneness of body and soul—at the appropriate time, then, open up that sealed garden so that he can drink from the fountain of you. Go nestle in his garden of nuts, and see if his pomegranates are in bloom![1]

The Bible celebrates sex when it is a passionate expression of deep, committed, lasting love between a man and a woman, love that grows greater with time.

> *O sons, listen to me. . . . Let your fountain be blessed, and rejoice in the wife of your youth, a lovely deer, a graceful doe. Let her breasts fill you at all times with delight; be intoxicated always in her love. (Proverbs 5:7, 18–19 ESV)*

There is noting better than being romanced.

The pursuit is part of the magic. When the Cowboy and I were dating, we were inflamed with desire for one another. But it was the waiting, the turning away from each other and separating ourselves so we could hold out for our wedding day, that increased the passion, the romance, the respect. We became one on our wedding day, not before. So marriage ever since has been an exploration of the beauty and wonder of sex, through good times and bad.

Sex has been a balm for us, a healing oil, through the most difficult times of our lives. And because it's private, because there is no shame, we are free to enjoy its fruits. God knows what we need from each other to feel secure.

Yada, the Hebrew word for sexual union, means to know, be known, and be deeply respected. To have sexual union with a man is to *know him* in the deepest sense. To know, to

---

1. Song of Songs 6:11

be known by him, to be respected, just as God knows and respects us. Just as God pursues us, waits for us, and then enters into a promise of His undying love with us.

Dating isn't knowing; it's the pursuit of knowing. It's wanting to know. It's *desiring* to know deeply, and this is good and healthy. But what the movies miss, what the media misses, is that *much of the romance is in the restraint.* I can't remember anything more attractive than my husband guarding my purity. When he stood up for it, protected it, and walked away from taking what should have been his in marriage only, I knew he was my soul mate. I saw through his actions that he had my best interest at heart. It wasn't just about physical union, but a heart *knowing*. And he *knew* my tender heart needed guarding.

That sex is a normal part of dating is a myth. Sex is an embrace of souls, the joining of lives, and it is the fabric on which God weaves a family.

So I charge you, by the does of the field, and even the gazelles, do not arouse or awaken love until the right *time*.

Finally, when you do get married, be creative and fun. Don't ever lose the flirting and fun you had when you were dating. When you have been married sixteen years like I have, there is never a better time to go out and get a new nightie, plan a fun date in a secluded place, have a picnic, and make some love. The couple in the Song of Songs had sex in a vineyard. They were sensual and sweet, alluring and adoring. But they never, ever physically dominated, bound, or belittled one another.

Before we wrap up the truths that replace this myth, I want to be honest with you about married sex. Sometimes it's the last thing you feel like doing. When you have babies who are pulling on you all day, bills spread like a choo-choo train on the counter, and in-law issues that are about to make you explode, and then you get in a big fight with your husband about who-knows-what, you aren't all that excited to get in a new nightie and explore the henna blossoms, if you know what I mean.

But you do it anyway. You do it because you know it's a healthy escape, it's healing balm, and it brings unity. If you have to take a long, hot shower to wash off the baby spit-up, run your head under the beating water to forget the bills, sugar scrub away the in-law drama, get down on your knees to forgive your husband for whatever he said that hurt you, and raise your heart to the heavens to hand over whatever ways you both have failed each other's expectations, then do it. Shave, put on lotion and his favorite perfume, and let the scent of your allure drift across the bed. Draw his heart to yours. Touch his body and let him know you are *for* him.

Make love and look into his eyes. It is called grace.

It is from this fabric that you stay stitched together.

Sex is best when it is safe, secure, and loving. At the right time, with the right person, under the blankets of God's good and holy love, you will experience grace in its finest form.

There is no fear in love. The only fear you will ever have is the fear that you are not enough and neither is he. But faith pushes past these fears and courage gets naked. Gets bare. Gives everything undone to heaven, and loves with passion and purity.

MYTH 18:

Guys Only Care about Looks.

(So that's what I'm focused on.)

—

TRUTH 18:

Genuine Beauty Wins a Prince's Heart.

(And we want love to last. . .)

LIFE VERSE:

Don't be concerned about the outward beauty of fancy hairstyles, expensive jewelry, or beautiful clothes. You should clothe yourselves instead with the beauty that comes from within, the unfading beauty of a gentle and quiet spirit, which is so precious to God.

1 PETER 3:3–4 NLT

A Cinderella Story

When I was a little girl, I watched *Cinderella* in the animated version, the images of the young princess in the soft blue gown drawn in stark contrast to her evil stepmother's sleek black skirt and wicked glare.

When the prince fell in love with her, Cinderella was actually in the middle of a very difficult story. Her real mother, as beautiful within as she was on the outside, had died; and her father married a wretch of a woman who lorded her authority over Cinderella. To compound matters, she had two jealous stepsisters; and if pretty is as pretty does, they were ugly. Cinderella's father died while away on a voyage, and she became a captive to her angry stepmother and self-centered sisters. Forced to wait on them hand and foot, Cinderella became a slave in her own home, dressed in rags, mopping floors and cleaning the fireplace—not even allowed to join them at the dinner table or enjoy a room of her own, but instead serving everyone else and sleeping in the cold, rustic attic.

One day, the mother and sisters noticed ash on Cinderella's face and laughed at the soot that had soiled her china-white cheek. Cattily, they named her Cinder-Ella, an addition to her given named of Ella. Laughing at her wickedly, these nasty sisters focused on their outward appearance: their dresses, sashes, makeup, jewels, gowns, hairdos, and heels. Rotting with envy, the mother hated Cinderella, degrading her own beauty. Jealousy and control transformed the mother's porcelain skin, lean build, and expensive clothes into symbols of evil.

Kindness and Courage

At the very beginning of the modern version of *Cinderella*, we witness a life-changing moment when her real mother plants three essential seeds in her heart. Lying on her deathbed, her gentle and benevolent mother summons her young daughter in to see her.

"I want to tell you a secret that will see you through all the trials that life can offer," her mother tells her. "Have courage and be kind. You have more kindness in your little finger than most people possess in their whole body. And it has so much power. For where there is kindness, there is goodness, and where there is goodness, there is magic."

As Cinderella's mother faces her death, she knows her daughter will have a wound in her heart. She rests her head on the pillow and whispers, "Forgive me," then closes her eyes.

No matter how wicked Cinderella's stepmother became, how selfish her sisters, how dismal her circumstances, Cinderella still sang and danced and found the good in her situation. When words were used against her, she didn't let them stick. Even when her stepmother squeezed her arm and told her she was "wretched"—Cinderella continued to live out of her primary identity: kindness and courage.

When the prince first happens upon her story, she is riding a horse, desperate to escape the cruelty in her home. Without a stitch of makeup, she meets her prince bare-faced and bare-hearted. Even then she tells him: have courage and be kind.

A true prince, he falls in love with the beauty of her heart for she had lived a life of kindness, courage, and forgiveness long before she met the prince.

When it comes time for the ball, her stepsisters obsessively ready themselves with makeup, hairdos, and fanciful gowns that are sure to garner the attention of the prince. But he is looking for the Cinderella he discovered on that fateful day in the forest—the one dressed in rags, whose genuine smile and kindhearted nature made her the most wanted woman in the kingdom.

Sometimes we think it's about our hair. Our makeup. Our weight. Our pimples. Our clothes. Our shape. Our shoes. The dishes we must do. The mopping. The chores. The loneliness of the attic. Sometimes we think it's all about us and how we feel and how we look—that all a guy looks at is the outside anyway—and he just wants someone to feast his eyes on, to get his hands on.

In truth, there are wolves disguised as princes; there are men who only want to take from women, who steal their identity and purpose by abusing their bodies and souls. But we are worth more.

Real princes look beyond our figures and at our hearts.

So the question remains with us: Are we focused on what people see, or are we cultivating a beauty that lasts? A beauty that has power far greater than anything we can offer physically? Are we gentle? Are we kind? Are we forgiving? Are we victims of our circumstances, or are we victors, knowing that we are loved? Are we real and unashamed? Are we honest? Are we faithful? Are we pure-hearted, or are we filled with jealousy, anger, and bitterness, spite that tastes sour in our mouths? Or is the teaching of kindness on our tongues?

Real princes admire the outward, but it is the *inward joy, peace, and true love* that have the power to keep their hearts closest to ours. When we are cruel or argumentative or conniving or bitter, they run away. But when we are sweet, we have them eating out of our palms.

Good men, husband-material men, look beyond the surface and want to know us *for who we are within*. They want to "know us deeply and respect us"—they want to *yada* us—they want to "know" and "be known." This is not the case with wolves. You must know the difference between a wolf and a hunter. A wolf wants to feast his eyes on you, steal, destroy, demolish, control, manipulate, convince, connive, diminish your value, and distract you from your purpose.

But the highest calling of a true prince is to point people toward the King—to help us find our security, joy, peace, and faith in God and not in men. When a man comes home at the end of the day, it is peace he wants to see in our eyes, not envy. It is strength he wants to perceive, not fear. It is faith in God and faith in them that keeps them attracted to us for life. It is knowing *their* fears and insecurities and *building them up* into the men they can become. It is knowing their lack and speaking gain into their souls. It is "grace upon grace."

Outward beauty that lacks inward grace will never keep a man's heart close to yours. Good men are deeply attracted to humility, a servant's heart, and most of all, an acceptance of *who he is* through and through.

When the prince comes for her hand, Cinderella humbly says to him, "Your majesty, I am no princess. I have no carriage, no parents, no dowry, and I do not even know if that beautiful slipper will fit. But if it does, will you take me as I am? An honest country girl who loves you."

"Of course I will," the prince replies. "But only if you will take me as I am: an apprentice still learning his trade."

Hence the deepest longing of a woman's heart, and a man's heart, too: to be accepted as we are. This is *yada*: "to know and be known."

He pursues her because he respects her. And of course

it would throw the whole story off if he snuck up to the attic and "knew" her then. No—the romance in it all is that he is patient in winning her. He searches the whole land to find her and refuses to settle for anything less than the best. When he finds her, he waits patiently for her to reciprocate his feelings, for her to confess her love as well. When she does, he politely asks for her hand in marriage and gives her the greatest gift any girl could desire—a lavish day of celebration, a pure and blissful wedding, and *then, and only then,* does he take her to the palace to be his lover and his bride, his companion at his side.

Ashes or a Crown?

Right before the prince and Cinderella exit her house for good, they turn and see her stepmother lurking on the stairs.

"I forgive you," Cinderella says to her, and she and the prince face forward and walk hand-in-hand directly into their future. The stepmother sinks into an ash heap.

We know that Cinderella could be bitter, but she chooses not to be. She certainly could have taken her mop bucket of bitterness right into her life with the prince. She could have wallowed in the soiled water of her life's circumstances, angry at her father, disappointed in her mother, furious at the years she spent pining away in lack while they lived in luxury. Her heart could have carried hatred for her sisters. She could have played a poor, sad victim her whole life through. But she picks victory; she picks the crown, and in her heart, she has worn one all along.

An example for us all, Cinderella refuses to let bitterness take root in her heart. She grants unasked-for, unmerited forgiveness to those who belittle and degrade her. For those she lost, she lives in love. These choices determined her future long before she could see it: she would wear the crown of the princess, and she would bring good to the prince and the kingdom with her genuine beauty.

Cinderella's mother taught her the secret to life—and the secret to a prince's heart. Kindness, courage, and forgiveness are the lasting qualities that make a woman beautiful, because they speak goodness and grace—and wherever there is goodness and grace, there is magic.

Don't wait until you see a prince on the horizon to *try* to become kind, forgiving, and courageous—by then it will be too late. These are virtues to practice now. As the Word says, "Who can find a virtuous wife? For her worth is far above rubies" (Proverbs 31:10 NKJV).

Be the princess before you meet the prince. If you need help—talk to a counselor or mentor; spend time in the Word getting to know Jesus' heart for you. If you need to, sort through your upbringing or the ways people have failed you—take the time to develop the internal qualities that make a woman beautiful. You are worth the time and investment it takes to cultivate a kind and forgiving spirit.

If you do this before you meet your prince, you won't bring a mop bucket full of dirty water into your marriage. You will live your life as a victor and a victim no more.

A girl who is kind now—no matter what unkindness is thrown her way—is beautiful beyond measure in the eyes of God and man. A woman who faces her greatest fear with courage—knowing who she is despite her circumstances—wears a crown no one can see but God and makes a great bride-to-be for a true prince. A young woman who practices the freedom of forgiveness every day will make a wonderful wife. If she doesn't become a wife, she'll make a great friend, great daughter, great mother, and great leader.[1]

Powerful Beauty

The world has it backward. We are taught to focus on the mirror, the makeup, the clothes, and pictures—and images that supposedly define us. I know what this is like—modeling was all about the size, shape, weight, look. The measurement of my figure was the measure of my worth.

But when I met the Cowboy, I met a man of distinct character. A man who was drawn to the interior qualities that make me beautiful—my gifts, my heart, my longing to be a good wife and mother. Yet I have found that no matter how hard I try, I cannot win him with a demanding attitude or contentious spirit. I cannot win him with arguments made with words. Being self-centered, rude, condemning, or contrary turns him completely off to me—he runs the other way.

As I heard a pastor once say, "When a woman speaks to me without honor, I cannot hear her."

Whatever season you are in right now—single and satisfied, hoping for marriage, or married—I wonder if this might be a time to cultivate the interior qualities that make a woman beautiful. It certainly is that time for me. We must hide this truth in our hearts and practice, bit by bit, living it out: it is the "gentle and quiet spirit" that is powerful in God's sight and wins a prince's heart for the good. And if these things don't come naturally for us,

1. If you need help with forgiveness, download my forgiveness worksheet at urmore.org/facts.php.

through open and honest confession before God we can become brighter and more beautiful as He transforms us to be more like Him.[2]

Kinder.

More courageous.

Gentler.

More good.

More loving.

More forgiving.

More selfless.

These are the essential ingredients of the healthy human spirit, and they are the simple qualities that win a man of good character.

In marriage, we can rest and trust in the headship of our husbands to protect and guide us, even if they are not believers, even if they have issues, even if they don't do everything right.

I remember on our wedding day, standing at the altar, grinning at the Cowboy when the pastor said that when hard times came, we were to remember the rings around our fingers as symbols of our promise. A foolish and young bride, I couldn't imagine that hard times would really come to us—we were so in love!

Well, guess what?

Hard times came.

Then they came again.

And again.

While I've stayed true to my promise I made on my wedding day and never stopped loving my prince, there have been times that I haven't been kind and haven't had one bit of courage, times I've needed to forgive and leave the mop bucket of ashes in my past. And this is done step

2. 2 Corinthians 3:18

by step, day by day with Jesus. I am always asking Him to show me how I can change and what I can do to be a better friend and lover.

So what's the secret to becoming a real-life Cinderella?

Becoming beautiful long before the ball, and continuing to beautify yourself afterward.

I'm not talking about your hair (hint, hint). I'm talking about genuine beauty—the kindness, the courage, the forgiveness that win princes, time and again.

It is our interior qualities of genuine friendship and love that are powerful to God and men, and we always do best when we take care of the outside but cultivate our inside to be far more remarkable than the clothes, watches, or purses we wear, the cars we drive, or the homes we live in. We were created by God to be reflections of His goodness.

Where there is goodness, there is kindness; and where there is kindness, there is magic. We have more power in the tip of our little finger than all that money can buy.

MYTH 19:

Singleness Is Waiting for Marriage.

(What you really need is a man.)

—

TRUTH 19:

Both Singleness *and* Marriage
Can Be Awesome.

(Make the most of what you have.)

LIFE VERSE:

How can a young person stay on the path of purity? By living according to your word. I seek you with all my heart; do not let me stray from your commands. I have hidden your word in my heart that I might not sin against you.

PSALM 119:9–11 NIV

Are You Satisfied?

We have the tale of two friends. One of them is grateful for everything she gets; the other always wants more. One of them doesn't need popularity to feel secure; the other questions her worth when people don't include her. One is joyful and free; the other is fearful and jealous. One is happy-go-lucky, and the other is tied in knots. One is walking on water; the other has everyone walking on eggshells.

They both find their soul mates and get married.

As married women, their circumstances change, but a whole lot doesn't change.

One is grateful for her little house and new job; the other wants a bigger house and more money. One doesn't need her husband's attention to feel happy; the other questions his love for her and demands his attention. One is surrounded by friends and family; the other has rocky relationships. One is leading her friends to the Lord; the other is trying to pick up the pieces from her last argument with her husband.

Two friends. Two very different stories.

Who you are today determines your destiny tomorrow.

Some women see singleness as a time to explore the world, grow their talents, impact their communities, and become the women God destined them to be. Others see it as a time to find a man. During my single years, I had a roommate who was getting married. I expressed my desire for marriage as well, and she told me I should concentrate on becoming the kind of woman who would attract the kind of man I so desired. True!

Singleness is a time to become that woman—not so that you can win a man, but so that you can become whole, fulfilled, at peace with who you are, and contribute to the world in meaningful ways.

As my friend Nancy puts it:

Our hearts don't change a lot on either side of the marriage or the singleness divide. I find that what's true of our hearts before we're married is generally true of women's hearts after they get married. So what we need to deal with is not so much how to change our circumstances, but how to let God change us in the midst of our circumstances, whatever they might be. [1]

Nancy's Story

Nancy DeMoss Wolgemuth was single for fifty-six years before she met her groom. At that age, she had no expectations to get married. She had spent her life very fulfilled in her relationship with Christ. Nancy had many friends, an active ministry, and rich, satisfying relationships. She fully expected that singleness was her calling and virtue. But when she met Robert, the Lord showed her that He had an unexpected blessing in store for her. Robert was a widower with an extended family of children and grandchildren. He, too, had lived a satisfying life apart from Nancy.

Nancy knew what the Bible said about singleness: "A woman who. . .has never been married can be devoted to the Lord and holy in body and in spirit. But a married woman has to think about her earthly responsibilities and how to please her husband" (1 Corinthians 7:34 NLT). As Paul wrote, "I want you to do whatever will help you serve the Lord best, with as few distractions as possible" (verse 35 NLT). That is exactly what Nancy did with her years as a single woman—she served the Lord with joy. She allowed His Word to counsel her. She loved

1. "Before I Become a Mrs. Day 1," ReviveOurHearts.com, November 11, 2015, https://www.reviveourhearts.com/radio/revive-our-hearts/i-become-mrs-day-1/.

her life as a single woman and made the very most of it—and she needed to be certain that God was redirecting her life.

As Nancy puts it, "The Lord had never awakened love for a man in my heart." So when Robert displayed interest in her, she told him that the Lord would have to stir up love in her heart, and He did. She fell deeply in love with Robert and gave herself to him in marriage, completely prepared to serve a husband with the same joy with which she had served Christ.

Unlike Nancy, many single women are bitter. They have longed for marriage their entire lives, and they have not found the right person. This can be very painful for women when their hearts' cry is to get married and have a family. But circumstances never bring the joy we think they will; it is our position of surrender and humbleness before the Lord, like Mary's, that brings the greatest joy. "I am the Lord's servant. May your word to me be fulfilled," Mary said to the angel—and these words were the ones Nancy chose for her life (Luke 1:38 NIV). In singleness she sought the Word as her guide; in marriage she would do the same.

I love how another woman in ministry, Lisa Harper, defines her singleness: "My husband is lost and hasn't stopped to ask for directions!" She says this with such joy, laughter, and exuberance that I guarantee you, if he ever finds his way to her, she is going to attract him like a sunbeam on a dark day.

Whether a woman is twenty-seven, thirty-seven, forty-seven, fifty-seven, or much older, being single and satisfied is possible.

When Nancy walked down the aisle, she did so with the same joy she had loved Jesus with her entire life. She submitted herself to His plan and received His gifts with gratitude. This makes a single woman joyful; this makes a married woman joyful; and we can all learn from her.[2]

2. To find out more about Nancy's ministry, go to reviveourhearts.com.

Singleness is a calling. Marriage is a calling. Our fulfillment comes from our relationship with Christ.

Like Nancy, Lisa Harper has spent her single years traveling and teaching others—and finally, in her forties, with no husband on the horizon, she sought to adopt a child. After a painful adoption attempt fell through, Lisa finally adopted a beautiful little girl from Haiti whose mama died of AIDS and who is HIV positive herself. Lisa loves that little girl with a single-minded devotion rare to women.

Singleness can be a gift, just as marriage can be a gift. It is not just a time of waiting for marriage—it is the "now" of your life, and you can make the most of it! Mary Magdalene, who followed Jesus to the cross and cried at His tomb, was single—and it was her singleness that allowed her this experience. Singleness is highly valued in scripture because it allows people a single-minded service to God without the distractions of family life. So present your requests to the Lord—pour out your desires to Him—let Him have the dreams of your heart and trust Him with the answer.

If you do hope to get married, this is a great time in your life—what time is better?—to take good stock of the interior qualities that make a woman beautiful. Study the Word, surround yourself with good friends, and serve. Have fun while you are single, and do the most with the time you have!

The Promise of Waiting

I want to make sure in this book that I don't promise women that if they stay sexually pure, they will have it all. That's a myth, too. God doesn't grant gifts on account of our remarkable righteousness. He grants gifts because we are His children and because He loves us.

Our righteousness is not from us; it is from Christ, and it is in devotion to Christ that we stay pure.

Sadly, the church has sometimes led women down a dead-end road by making promises that people can't make. Here's the promise: if you take this road (sexual purity), it will lead to a prince, and then when you hop in bed with the prince, you will be rolling around in a pot of gold (sexual ecstasy).

But women who wrote me their stories said they wished they hadn't stayed pure for the promise of "the greatest sex ever," but instead had stayed pure out of simple devotion to Christ. Many of them got married as virgins and felt insecure and nervous in bed. Because of their huge expectations for unbelievable intimacy and sexual climax after climax, they felt frustrated, disappointed, and unlovely because it wasn't that way at all.

A friend of mine, Heather, wrote:

> I was a good girl, the grew-up-in-the-church type. And there was a promise for girls like me. If you wait till you get married to have sex, then everything will be wonderful. After finding Prince Charming, waiting bought my ticket to Happily-Ever-After in the arena of sex.
>
> Only, it didn't quite work out that way. Sex was difficult, awkward, even uncomfortable for me most of the time during those early months. I felt betrayed by God—like He hadn't kept His end of the bargain and made my sex life great as a reward for waiting. I blamed all of our sexual issues on my husband—because he did not wait—believing he had somehow stolen the reward from our marriage. I wondered if I should have made marrying a virgin a bigger priority.
>
> Now, after a decade of marriage, I can discern

that our adjustment to married life and sex was common. I can also recognize a harder truth: I waited for the sake of following a rule and hoping for a reward. My waiting was nothing more than a religious action. It had nothing to do with wanting to stand holy before God, nor did it stem from wanting to honor God with my body.

Had my desire been to keep my dating relationships holy—instead of just "sex-free"—my experience transitioning to married sex may have been different.

I wish that "waiting" hadn't come with the promise of awesomeness. I wish I had waited simply out of obedience to God, not because I thought I would get "better gifts" that way. That put undue strain on our young marriage.

Heather is not alone. It is not easy for women to keep that garden sealed and then to think that in one day it's going to transform into a lush vineyard of delights. Learning your husband's body and him learning yours takes lots and lots of practice—years and years! So when and if you get married, take the pressure of performance off each other and don't expect perfection. Great sex between a married couple is a process. It takes grace, time, and the investment of both people to achieve the kind of intimacy we long for.

My friend Beckie and her husband met when they were kids, began dating at sixteen, and married at nineteen. Beckie writes:

It was very hard to wait, but we are so glad we did. We had known for years this was the person we wanted to marry, and that's part of what made the waiting so hard. Never having sex, it was a rocky start (mostly for me), but we always said (and still say), we have lots more years to keep working on it. We are thankful that we are the only person the other has ever even kissed.

Pressure's Off!

If there is one thing this book does for you, I hope you come to know the treasure of your sexuality and the impact of your sexual choices on your life. As my mentor, Devi, always tells me, the choices you make today will determine your destiny tomorrow.

Here's one last story from a woman who waited. You'll see that all the pressure is off when you take it off, when you let go and let God write your story. Here's Andrea:

> *I grew up in a Christian home. My parents didn't speak much of intimacy or sex other than we were to wait for marriage. I remember hearing about a best friend's first experience when we were freshmen in high school. I was kind of shocked and had a feeling of sadness and devastation listening to her recount what happened. Sex was supposed to be shared between a husband and wife. I couldn't understand how my friends could give themselves away so easily and with little to no commitment to each other.*
>
> *As I grew up, more and more of my friends were experimenting with sex, and some of them were being intimate with countless guys. I didn't attract attention like they did, and I was glad. I decided that I would remain a virgin until I was married not only to please my parents, but to please God. I also wanted to weed out the "bad guys" who wanted*

to date me for the wrong reasons.

I had my first kiss when I was seventeen, the summer before college. I was embarrassed that it had taken me so long to actually meet a guy who wanted to kiss me, and I was glad it finally happened—and now that I look back on it—I wish I would have just waited entirely for when I met my husband.

Dating guys in college was challenging. I often dated men who "put up with" my virginity for a few weeks, sometimes a few months, and then they would drop me because I wouldn't have sex with them. I remember one guy specifically that I will never forget. We stopped dating after three months. After we were finished dating, he was speaking with a friend of his about me and didn't know I was a few steps away and could hear their conversation. His friend asked him why we weren't together.

His response was, "She's a virgin, and with this thing (points to his private parts) and her first time, can you imagine?" And they laughed and laughed. I was so hurt and left the party. Sex was only about the chase to him, as it was with the majority of the men I dated in school.

I would hear of my friends giving their virginity away to random guys, and then they would never hear from these men again. I knew I wanted to be different. I was worth more.

I remember dating and praying to God to bring me a good guy, a man who loved God and listened to His Word. I would often journal these prayers and pray for my future husband.

When I met my husband, right away I knew he was different. He didn't pressure me to have physical intimacy. Instead, he tried to learn about my mind and my heart.

My husband and I got married three and a half years into our dating relationship. In all honesty, our wedding night was rough. We ended up not having sex that night—I was too worked up. I had friends that were cheering me on as we left. "Have fun tonight!" they called, and it's hard for a girl like me to have that kind of pressue. My husband and I decided to sleep and try in the morning, and that was successful. I remember speaking with my mom that morning and saying, "I'm not a virgin anymore!" as tears fell off my cheeks. I was proud of myself, and it was a moment of gratefulness to God for protecting me all through those years of dating.

Now that I have children of my own, I can only hope and pray that they choose to remain pure until they get married as well. My husband and I didn't take the same path as each other, and that's okay. There's no judgment, only love. That's what we will hopefully pass down to our kids as well.

How Does a Young Woman Stay Pure?

The Bible says a young person stays pure by living according to God's Word. The Word of God has that much power to guide your life choices! Seek God with all your heart. Run in the path of His commands. Let His Word be your light and guide.

Here are some simple guidelines to help you:

Do:

♥ Spend time daily in God's Word and prayer, giving thanks and pouring out your heart's desires as a lifetime practice.

♥ Go to church, Bible study, youth group, or women's groups on a regular basis—surround yourself with a healthy community that upholds sexual purity and celebrates both singleness and marriage.

♥ If you date someone, talk to him about your commitment to purity. If that is not his commitment, this may not be the right relationship for you. Be open to God's leading to find the person He has for you.

♥ When dating, stay in public places. If you choose to kiss, stay where others can see you—front porches are great for this!

♥ Decide in advance to keep your clothes on; plan ahead that everything stays zipped, buttoned, and fastened.

♥ Dress modestly so no one is tempted to see you as more of a body than a soul.

♥ Guard your eyes, mind, and heart from sexual impurity on the screen. Decide not to feast your eyes (the windows of your soul) on sexual immorality or anything that makes you struggle with your purity.

Don't:

♥ Take any drink or drug that would weaken your defenses.

♥ Look at pornography or engage in sexual websites.

♥ Be alone with a date in a bedroom, parked car, or other compromising place.

♥ Think you can do this alone—remember your community and connection with other Christ-followers will give you the support you'll need to resist sexual temptation.

♥ Confuse sexual purity with a religious law you have to follow to earn a blessing; instead, choose sexual purity as an outpouring of your love for the Lord.

MYTH 20:

Sex Is What We Want.
(And more of it!)

—

TRUTH 20:

Love Is What We Need
(May you find that your cup runneth over.)

LIFE VERSE:

*"Love one another,
even as I have loved you."*

JOHN 13:34 NASB

Raising the Bar

The Cowboy's dad, whom we affectionately call Papa, was a very successful businessman in his day. Papa once held a campaign in his office called "Raise the Bar." He challenged his colleagues to take everything up a notch, to not just measure up to their own standard of "best," as they had been doing, but to take their best and lift it even higher. That campaign led to one of the company's most fruitful years, and the mission stuck. To this day, the people Papa mentors know to "raise the bar"—to take their standard of best and shoot higher.

When we talk about sex, we have to raise the bar. Is it sex we really want? Or is it love in the finest form? What truly fills the aches of the human heart? Is it to "know" and "be known"? To love and be loved? To hope, and to hope together? Or is it just to have sex?

The truth is, there are men who just want sex, and the girl gives it away thinking she will receive the love she needs. But then he's done with her. He doesn't want to marry her or take her home to Mama. And the girl is left heartbroken.

On the other end of the spectrum, real men respect real women's bodies and the ways their hearts are connected to them. Real men—husband-material men—are the ones who are raising the bar when it comes to sex, and saying, "I want more than that. What I really want is a companion for life. A best friend. A soul-knowing. And I'm willing to wait to find that."

As women, we get to decide who we are going to be: the ones giving sex to get love (which doesn't work), or the ones who raise the bar and stand for love in its finest form, knowing true love is willing to wait for the right time.

Sex without love is meaningless. It cheapens the mystery.

In its deepest meaning, sex is an expression of unity

laced by grace. It is, as the Bible describes, "the mystery of Christ and the church." For without grace, there is no reunion of souls between Jesus and His bride. Without mercy, forgiveness, acceptance, there is no entry to heaven.

To raise the bar is to say that sex is holy. It is not just physical; it is emotional; it is spiritual; it is an expression of love, the completion of married love, the most beautiful union of bodies and souls that one can experience on earth. Next to that is the mystery of a child in the womb and at her mother's breast.

Sex is a mercy-lined mystery too sacred to explain, a creation of a romantic God. It is wrong to cheapen sex with flippant lyrics or paint it as profane in videos, or put a price tag on it, or steal it by force. And it is wrong to treat sex as commonplace. In the words of Solomon,

> *There are three things which are too wonderful for me, yea, four which I know not: the way of an eagle in the air; the way of a serpent upon a rock; the way of a ship in the midst of the sea; and the way of a man with a maiden. (Proverbs 30:18–19 ASV)*

We raise the bar when we say that the union of a man with a maiden is as mysterious as an eagle soaring in the sky. Sex is as powerful as a ship traveling the vast and dangerous sea. No person can comprehend the mystery of the serpent on the rock. The way of a man with a maiden is the way of grace, of beauty and desire and unity. It represents our need for restoration, reconciliation, reunion. It is the way of Christ with us, no less.

To raise the bar is to say our bodies are temples. We are not for sale; nor are we for free.

What Is Love?

There is this standard of love that the Old Testament teaches: "'Love the Lord your God with all your heart, and with all your soul, and with all your mind'. . . . 'Love your neighbor as yourself' " (Matthew 22:37, 39 NIV). That's a high standard. First, to love God with everything we are—our emotions, thoughts, physical strength—through the good, bad, aching, and ugly; to love Him wholly; to praise Him through suffering and loss; to hold Him high through it all, despite it all, because of it all. And then to turn around and love our neighbors as ourselves: love like this requires sacrifice and commitment.

The Cowboy is good at this. You will often catch him in the street talking to our neighbors. From what I've seen (and what I want to live out), love loves even when they are different than us and we don't know them well, even when they are weak or sick or lonely or rejected, even when their lives appear Facebook happier than ours. It means going beyond ourselves, taking the lead, the hands and feet of grace.

A former neighbor of ours named Cathi was beaten as a child, battered by two husbands, stunned by the tragic death of both of her children, and it seemed she always had a ready smile. She didn't walk as a victim; she knew her Lord Jesus and walked in victory and trust. In fact, she had a funny little habit of leaving little boxes with minuscule mustard seeds in them on the tables of coffee shops and in bathrooms where she thought people needed encouragement. She was a joyful lady who had known deep sorrow that birthed in her the deep things of God—Cathi knew that people just need a little mustard seed, the tiniest in the world, to grow big faith.

She lived a life of gratitude and never asked for much; she always gave to the sick neighbors, the beaten and broken down, and did it quietly without needing anyone to know. In fact, the only reason I know about how she loved everybody in our little mountain neighborhood during those years is because everyone else would tell me how she brought a basket of groceries and never left a note—but we all knew it was the angel on 3rd Street, who had battled through her own personal pain on knees worn from prayer and gave her life as an offering to many.

To love your neighbor the way you love yourself—that's a high bar to reach for, and few of us live it. When we love like that, we become Jesus with skin on. We talk to our neighbors. We get to know them. We care about their stories and their pain. We lay down our own needs for their good. In our self-centered worlds it seems impossible. But what a beautiful thing it is to go next door to see if the girl who lives there needs a friend, someone to laugh with or cry to. There is no end to this call to love. One could spend a lifetime serving her neighbors without the job ever really being finished. People always need more love, and there are always more people to love. To love like this takes meekness, no need to be seen. It is from the heart. It loses self. It must be the highest calling of man.

But guess what? Jesus raises the bar. Jesus takes the Old Testament command to love our neighbors as ourselves and lifts it higher: "'A new command I give you: Love one another. As I have loved you, so you must love one another'" (John 13:34 NIV).

Now that's a high jump of a whole new height.

That's a Cathi kind of love. To look beyond your own struggles and figure out what your neighbor needs. To offer a ready smile; to leave a seed of faith that can move a mountain; to love the way Jesus loves. Now that's raising the bar.

A Confession

I have discovered something in the writing of this book: I have a lot of head knowledge about God. I know a lot of verses—and now I know a lot of verses about sex!

That is good, but it is not enough.

I love the Lord with all my heart, mind, soul, and strength.

That is good, but it is not enough.

I am still discovering what it is to love my neighbor, to love others as Jesus loves us. I want the love Jesus has for me to flow into the way I love others. But to do that, I have to reach beyond my own feelings.

To truly "love others as Jesus loves me" would be amazing growth in my life, and I'm going after it. He raised the bar, and I know we can reach it for two reasons: first, I've seen love like this in action; and second, Jesus would never give us a challenge we couldn't reach.

Cathi has every right to sit at home and cry and not take her neighbor's call. God gave her a raw deal, right?

No. She chooses to *love* right there in the battle. She runs to her neighbor's aid. She lights the world.

One day Cathi's shoulders are surely going to sprout wings and she will fly like an angel. When Cathi laughs, our hearts become sure Jesus is going to walk right through the door and say *it is finished.*

I have hope in the eyes for just having known her.

This is the love we're after. This is the bar we're reaching for.

It's good to love God and love our neighbors, but it's great to love others as He has loved us. For if we have not love, we gain nothing.[1]

We can have the greatest sex in the world, but if we have not love, we gain nothing. It is a lie that women get love by giving sex. No, we get love by being filled with Christ.

When we have love, then we have faith. We believe. We hope, and hope never leaves us. We see God in the losses; we seek His face. We don't wear the sad face; we choose joy. We pick blessing. We find what we are grateful for—we hunt—and count. We thank God. We don't stop thanking Him. Our voices rise in praise even when we can't see clearly where the hope is, because we believe it's coming; we know it's there.

When we live like this—we live faith, hope, and love, and the greatest of these is love. We have so much more than sex. What we have endures forever; our cup runneth over.[2]

1. 1 Corinthians 13:3
2. Psalm 23:5

MYTH 21:

I Will Marry Prince Charming.

(And he will be perfect!)

—

TRUTH 21:

No Prince Is Perfect.

(But love can be.)

LIFE VERSE:

Let love be your highest goal!

1 CORINTHIANS 14:1

Moving Forward

Papa, eyes glistening grace, once winked at me and said, "You aren't married for forty-five years without knowing how to get creative, you know!" He turned toward his beloved, took her hand, and swept her off to someplace fun. Their marriage is a covering over our family. They are a couple who hit storms wide and long, who know what love is. They have stayed true to their God, their vows, their hearts, their family.

Love is. . .

♥ Love is patient and kind. Love is not jealous or boastful or proud or rude. It does not demand its own way. It is not irritable, and it keeps no record of being wronged. It does not rejoice about injustice but rejoices whenever the truth wins out. Love never gives up, never loses faith, is always hopeful, and endures through every circumstance. (1 Corinthians 13:4–7)

♥ Love never ends. (1 Corinthians 13:13)

♥ "Greater love has no one than this, that someone lay down his life for his friends." (John 15:13 ESV)

♥ This is real love—not that we loved God, but that he loved us and sent his Son as a sacrifice to take away our sins. (1 John 4:10)

♥ If we love each other, God lives in us, and his love is brought to full expression in us. (1 John 4:12)

♥ God is love, and all who live in love live in God, and God lives in them. And as we live in God, our love grows more perfect. . . . We love each other because he loved us first. (1 John 4:16–17, 19)

One time Papa told me a funny story. He and Linda had gotten in a big blowup when they were young marrieds. Angry, he sped off alone in his truck and drove away to their ranch to clear his head, an hour away. Just like the Cowboy, he found solitude in the country and went off in the woods to hack at trees. As darkness fell over the field, he returned to the ranch house, sweaty, grimy, worn tired, a man alone.

He walked into his bedroom, and there was Linda lying between the sheets waiting for him. "Beautiful Linda," he said, tipping his hand. A grin passed over his lips, fondness in the memory.

Sometimes a man and his wife work it out between the sheets. The ways they long, the things they want, the letting go and loving anyway. It's holy unity; it's not "sex"—that's almost a profane word for what really means "whole knowing."

Whole knowing is to accept one another in spite of your frailties, to throw each other a lifeline when the other is in the quicksand, to be the tender voice calling from the shore, to pull one another out of the sinking by saying through kisses and caresses that you are *for each other no matter what.*

In our closet we hung a sign that says: Forever and Always and No Matter What.

No matter what.

In the interior of the wedding bands we wear, the circle pressing against skin, these words are inscribed: Forever and Always.

Perfect Love

Love is the one thing that will fill your cup, that will keep you from living in constant fear, that will free you to live a life that runneth over.

When you search the Bible for the English word *sex*, you come up zero. When you search for *love*, you see it more than eight hundred times. Sex is *yada*. Sex is "knowing fully" as we are known by God.

I hunt for love, eight hundred times, more. It is in Jesus' lowering of Himself to lift us from the pit that we find love's truest tones.

It is in the love that God has for me that I want to fully live. Love is the manna we eat; the mystery in the bread as dew on the grass, the nourishment He provided when His people needed Him to carry them and trust Him with their tomorrows.

But even when He gave them their daily bread, they complained it was not enough—they wanted meat, they wanted more.

We women are prone to complain about the men we love, that what they provide is not enough; we want more— as if princes are God.

But surely, to love is to know the difference between a man and his Maker; to turn the palms up and let go; to trust that all that falls into our hands is a gift. Love says thank you for the manna, resides in today, and believes His faithfulness will be there tomorrow.

"It is better to take refuge in the LORD than to trust in princes" (Psalm 118:9 ESV).

To love is to thank, to bow low, to lift another higher. To believe in your beloved. Wait. Put trust in God. Surrender.

And to be kind.

We needn't hunt for love's definition; it's no mystery.

Love Is Patient

The Cowboy steps onto the front porch in the early morning; the hunter always sees what appears not to be there. On the surface, I see woods. Dimensions of trees, wildflowers speckling hay. Rain drizzling, fall morning mist. . . and he sees a buck. He points. I look, squint, glasses not yet on make the morning foggier. Camo clad, jacket big, rifle propped, he beckons, "Come, see."

I peer through morning mist up the trail to the right, and there is the buck, strong and sure, right where I saw nothing, gazing at us, standing majestic.

We catch our breath; still. Wait.

To hunt is to be a patient warrior, to stay in wait for what you cannot see, to trust that the reward of waiting will far surpass the discomfort, the cold, the stiffness, the hunger.

Love is the perfect kind of patient. If he shot at anything that crossed by, gave in to the trigger for the want of the kill, he would damage these woods that are our refuge. He would kill off young life. In love, we don't shoot to kill; we don't spray bullets for the hope of just one hit. We wait. We are sure of what we cannot see, that the wait is worth the feverish desire for what we want so badly.

In sex, we wait. We do not awaken love until just the right time. At the right time, we undress. It's a beautiful mystery—the pursuit of love, the wedding ring, the aisle to groom, the celebration, the wedding, the party, the wave good-bye, the bed, holy.

We must hunt for love.

In marriage we must be patient. We may want him to change like a hunter wants his kill, but we are there to help. God did not create him to complement us; he created us to complement him, to help him. There will be things the prince does not do well and things you do not know he needs. There will be messes and confusion and fights, and there will be long nights lingering over what was said, the "not enough" of who you are, the lack—and the more you fill the lack with lack, the darker your heart will become.

The lack has to be filled with Christ, always.

Love wakes early to pray for him. Rises early to serve, stays up late to *know and be known*. Love prepares for his homecoming with something refreshing to drink and a laugh.

And for the things that you are working on to change about you, and the things God is working to change in him, love hunts. Love doesn't spout off every bullet you can think of in hopes of reaching the target you want; love sees beyond what doesn't appear to be there and believes for the moment it will appear, a buck on a pathway in the surprise of morning light.

Love Is Kind

When the Cowboy and I got married, my grandfather gave us the advice to "be kind to one another." He came down our aisle in a wheelchair. His face was aged and worn when he said it. Grandpa is long gone, but his words still whisper: "Be kind."

My grandfather's first wife, my mother's mother, was not known for kindness.

Love isn't an angry snarl or a cutting truth or a shout—it's the brisk morning, sunrise shafting light through branches: *A harsh word stirs up anger but a gentle answer turns away wrath; rash words are like sword thrusts, but the tongue of the wise brings healing. An excellent wife does her husband good and not harm all the days of her life; the law of kindness is on her tongue.*[1]

---

1. Proverbs 15:1; 12:18, 31:10–12, 26

Words can blast the kindness right off the walls, and a man will go running; my grandpa left her when my mother was three.

Sometimes Grandpa's whisper can't be heard over our shouts. I'd rather paint a picture of a perfect prince charming and castles and walls laced with grace; I'd as soon tell you that if you wait like we did, even if you don't, there is going to be this happily-ever-after that is the gold-standard-of-love as surely promised as the band on his finger.

But then I'd be making promises no man can make, and this book is about truth.

It's a myth the prince will be perfect and you will be, too.

You are going to be human, and so will he.

The real promise of gold, the circle that never ends, is written here:

> *Let all bitterness and wrath and anger and clamor and slander be put away from you, along with all malice. Be kind to one another, tenderhearted, forgiving one another, as God in Christ forgave you. (Ephesians 4:31–32 ESV)*

Bitterness can grow anywhere—in marriages where there is plenty of health, plenty of children, plenty of wealth. There are women right now with loving husbands, healthy children, and beautiful homes in great neighborhoods who are wrestling bitterness to the ground with gratitude, thrashing about for joy, searching the woods for wisdom. It does not take a hard life to make a hard woman.

Then there are women who have not an inkling of bitterness in their war-torn souls, women who have been stripped of what we might consider rightful blessings for the upright in heart.

Looking at me with eyes clear as the morning, Cathi makes a circle with her forefinger and thumb and holds it up to her eye, peers through, dawn in the whites. "Zero bitterness," she reminds me.

What is the secret?

And why are we asking in a book about sex?

Because we are raising the bar on love—'cause love is what we really want—and there's nothing worse than a bitter woman in bed. Even if she is having sex, she is as far away from her man as the upstairs room, gripping the pillow angrily.

Whether she is gripping the pillow or gripping her Bible or gripping her fists or gripping her man, a bitter woman is rottenness in his bones. *An excellent wife is a crown to her husband, but one who brings shame is a cancer.*[2] She was made from his rib, his side, his bone. She is the marrow, the life. Eve's name means "life"—and we are the life of our husbands.

It is good for you, whatever your stage of life, to learn it now. From the beginning woman had the power to give man dignity and authority, a crown on his head; or to be a cancer. For a man would rather live in a desert alone than with a quarrelsome, complaining, nagging wife.[3]

But he who finds a good wife has found favor with God.[4]

If you want to know and be known, to love and be loved, you must rid yourself of the cancer so it doesn't spread into anyone else's bones.

Getting rid of bitterness means dealing with it—pulling the small roots out before they become nasty vines that choke life—and forgiveness is always the antidote. Bitterness is missing the grace of God, the gifts, the manna—the daily giving. It poisons like sexual sin poisons. It defiles. Stains. Eats away. So, as women in search of true beauty and true love, we mustn't miss the grace of God.

2. Proverbs 12:4
3. Proverbs 21:19
4. Proverbs 18:22

Here's the gold standard, as pure as the wedding band: no cruel words. No rash talk. Gentleness. Kindness, Forgiveness. Love. Thanks. Joy.

That's the bar, and we're shooting for it. We are not going to be perfect at it—many times we'll miss the mark—but as our heavenly Father is perfect and He lives in us and we abide in Him, it is possible.

Oh, and if you want me to bring it back to sex, you'll have better sex, more sex, and your sex will be pure, because before you even climb into bed you'll have forgiven whatever the day has brought and thanked God for all the graces. And in this, we will love as He has loved us.

Love Is Not Proud

The other day my counselor suggested I eat a piece of humble pie. She suggested it as if she were offering me a piece of chocolate pie on Thanksgiving Day. She made it sound so attractive that I wanted to gobble it up, like humble pie is the most delicious dessert ever.

She also suggested I put on my big-girl panties and say I'm sorry. She said it friend to friend, kind of like an inspirational speech before a big match. The way she said it made big-girl panties seem like a good thing, like they would help me do the right thing and be strong and eat my pie and everything really would be okay—especially if I admitted where I was at fault.

Humble. Pie.

Big. Girl. Panties.

It takes a big girl to eat her humble pie!

We know from the best description of love on the planet that "love is not. . .proud" (1 Corinthians 13:4 NLT). This is big-girl-panty stuff; it's not for the immature. So put on your panties and let's talk about love, because love is what you want, and love is really all you need.

In our family, we make chocolate pie for Thanksgiving, Christmas, and any time someone needs some extra love. It's sweet, it's rich, it's light, and the crust melts in your mouth. When topped with fresh whipped cream, it's pretty much perfection in a pie.

Love is the chocolate version of the humble pie. A humble person is also able to see how he or she has offended someone else. A humble person can admit her own wrongs.

Pride, on the other hand, is the biggest destroyer of love. Prides says, "I am right and you are wrong. I know better than you, and I am going to tell you how wrong you are!"

Humility says, "I respect your needs and desires. I want to hear your heart so that I can bless you. I want to know you and respect you deeply. What you think and experience is more important to me than how I feel right now. How can I help you?"

Jesus set us an example of humility. He had every right to come down to earth and point out everyone's sins, and to insist that He was right and everyone else was wrong. Instead, He came as a servant, setting an example of lowly love, loving in a manner that left the other person higher. Our need for a Savior mattered more to Him than how He felt. Our need came first to Jesus.

Linda always says:

Jesus first

Others second

Yourself last. . .makes JOY. And she has joy. No wonder she raced down highway 71 to beat Papa back to the ranch house that night. Loving him mattered more than being right.

To love, and I'm learning here, is to think of others more highly than yourself. To care for them more than you care for your own comfort. To offer to help. To say you're sorry when you're wrong.

To eat your humble pie like a big girl and make it taste sweet for everyone.

Love Keeps No Record of Wrongs

Love marks the ticket "paid in full." That means there is no list of all the things others have done to hurt you, disappoint you, fail you, assail you. And if you keep a list in your mind and it keeps getting longer, you can burn it.

Or you can list all the hurts and offenses and then one by one by one, write, PAID, PAID, PAID until the whole list is marked PAID IN FULL.

You can even write it in red letters if you like.

Or the sand.

Whatever it takes, mark others' debts PAID.

Lay the prince's sins at the cross.

That way when the dawn comes and you look your lover in the eyes, he'll want to wake up next to you day after day to see the light.

No Prince Is Perfect

When we married, I saw my Cowboy as the vision of perfection (which he is if you just look at him! He is soooo handsome!). But what I found out is no prince is perfect, but love can be. The worst times have been the times when I have expected him to be God and trusted in man instead of Christ.

The best times have been when I have raised my hands upward and let God be the artist painting the canvas of our future and rested in the Creator's hands.

We have a true Prince who is coming back for us one day, who loves us perfectly, without fail. The best thing we can do is lean in and listen for His still, small voice. Listen well. Love much. Fear nothing. Believe for more.

With Special Thanks

This book would not have been possible without the courageous men and women who shared their stories with me and allowed me to share them with you. Special thanks goes to Shane, Papa, Linda, Boo, Wendy, Dan, Bethany, Adam, Judah, Paige, Caleb, Devi, Nikki, Annie, Kimmie, Nancy, Heather, Beckie, Andrea, and Cathi. May your stories help us live better, stronger, and wiser. Thank you to the prayer team who prayed me through: Val, Megan, and Caris. Thanks to Trina, Michelle, Holly, and Kelly, who believed in me at the beginning and helped me at my wits end. And thank you to the incredible team at Barbour Publishing who believed in this book, and to Greg Johnson, my agent. Finally, thank You to my Lord and Savior, Jesus Christ, who makes all things new. I love You with all my heart!

About the Author

Jennifer Strickland is a woman saved by grace who seeks to walk in truth. She is married to her best friend, Shane, "the Cowboy." They live with their three precious children, Olivia, Zach, and Samuel, in north Texas. She is the author of several books and Bible studies and loves speaking in schools, prisons, and places where people are looking for more. To learn more about her ministry and discover resources that teach value and inspire purpose, go to www.urmore.org.

For more valuable resources related to *21 Myths (Even Good) Girls Believe about Sex*, go to 21myths.com.